HUMANISTIC PSYCHOLOGY

HUMANISTIC PSYCHOLOGY

A Christian Interpretation

JOHN A. HAMMES

Professor of Psychology
The University of Georgia

GRUNE & STRATTON
New York — London

*To my parents in the year of
their fiftieth wedding anniversary*

Grune & Stratton, Inc.
757 Third Avenue
New York, New York 10017

Library of Congress Catalog Card Number: 76-110448
International Standard Book Number: 0-8089-0650-X

Printed in the United States of America (PC-B)

Preface

The primary purpose of this book is to present the compatibility of scientifically established psychological truth with the truths proposed by a Christian frame of reference. A secondary purpose is to indicate the necessity for psychology to study not only human behavior but also the variables from which this behavior stems, variables that lie within the person.

Teilhard de Chardin, in his *Phenomenon of Man*, pointed out that the fundamental distinction between man and other animal life, in the tortuous course of evolution, is man's capability for reflection, which Teilhard defined as consciousness turning back upon itself. He further urged that the study of man, to be complete, must include the analysis of this reflective capability. And to the traditional Christian cross-sectional analysis of the essence or being of man, there must be added the dimension of time, or duration, in the study of evolving human consciousness. Man, according to Teilhard, is standing on the threshold of a great awakening, and the future of the universe is contained in the direction toward which human consciousness chooses to evolve.

It would appear, therefore, that scientific psychology has been caught in its own web of objectivity. In the attempt to reduce the study of man to stimulus-response behavior, scientific psychology has precluded the most important aspect of all, human consciousness. Psychology must shift its focal point, if it is to keep pace with evolutionary science.

The present text is a Christian synthesis of man's origin, purpose, and destiny. It also portrays the compatibility of Christian tradition with science. Speaking simply, a good scientist can be a good Christian, and a good Christian an excellent scientist.

This book has been written for the college student with little or no background in philosophy or theology. In conjunction with the Suggested Readings at the end of each part, the book can be used as a text for courses in humanistic psychology, personality, adjustment, mental hygiene, motivation, rational psychology, psychology of mind, and general philosophy of human nature. In summary, it gives a basic Christian orientation that can be expanded by the reader in any preferential development of a Christian theory of human nature.

The non-Christian reader may find himself in agreement with much of what is written in certain parts of the book, particularly if his psychological viewpoint is humanistically inclined. It should be noted, therefore, that a position held by a Christian psychologist is often held by a non-Christian as well, since a communality of agreement can often be reached on philosophical grounds that do not involve differentiating theological factors.

The text is divided into four parts. In Part I the basic methods available for the study of man are presented, with an evaluation of the place of operationism and relativism in psychological theory. In Part II various theories of the nature of man are examined, together with an analysis of human life-structure, thought, and choice behavior. The contribution of evolution to the explanation of man's origin is included. Part III is concerned with personal adjustment, in terms of man's interaction with his environment. Contemporary anxiety and guilt are studied, with an analysis of the factors helpful to healthy physical, intellectual, social, moral, and emotional growth. Part IV presents a Christian interpretation of the origin, purpose, and destiny of man. The problem of God's existence is examined, and his relationship to man is explored. Finally, at the end of each part, supplementary readings are suggested.

The author invites reader criticism of this work, whether positive or negative. Of course, constructive criticism and suggestions for improvement or inclusion of additional topics will be of greater value than the mere identification of inadequacies. The reader can be assured that comments will receive careful consideration.

The author recognizes a debt to his many teachers, both Christian and non-Christian, who have influenced the adoption of the philosophy underlying the present work. Any credit this book may merit should be attributed to them; any shortcomings are the fault of the author.

Acknowledgment is also due Miss Betty Wilker for her efficient typing of the manuscript, to Mrs. Mary Beussee and Mrs. Catherine Hoffman for their careful editing, and to the author's wife for her patient proofreading. Lastly, a perpetual debt is owed the author's parents, who in the entirety of their lives have exemplified the Christian ideals of love and sacrifice. To them this book is gratefully and lovingly dedicated.

J.A.H.

Contents

List of Tables

List of Figures

PART I

BASIC PRINCIPLES

In Chapter 1, by way of introduction, the contemporary state of man is presented from different perspectives. The three subsequent chapters establish ground rules and investigative approaches. Chapter 2 presents three traditional sources of information concerning man: science, philosophy, and religion. The influence of positivism and relativism in psychology is also discussed. Once methods are established, there remains the question of trustworthiness of their human application. Chapter 3 evaluates the validity of human certitude, a problem basic to determining the confidence that can be placed in human powers of discerning reality. Next, Chapter 4 examines the kinds of variables that can be legitimately inferred in psychological investigation. The recognition of causality is seen to be indispensable to a realistic theory of psychology.

Chapter 1

Contemporary Man

"Man has considered himself the earth's master since his species was established. After teasing out nature's secrets with incredible patience and ingenuity from the subatomic structure of matter to the dynamics of galaxies; after analyzing the composition of stars all but infinitely distant; after creating a world of comfort never dreamed of in fairy tales, it is perhaps paradoxical that he is still asking, 'Who am I?'"[1] This quotation from the preface of Severin's *Humanistic Viewpoints in Psychology* (1965) provides an apt introduction to this chapter.

ROBOTIZED MAN

Bertalanffy, in a work entitled *Robots, Men, and Minds* (1967), observes,

Psychology, in the first half of the twentieth century, was dominated by a positivistic-mechanistic-reductionistic approach which can be epitomized as the *robot model of man....* Basic for the interpretation of animal and human behavior was the *stimulus-response scheme* or, as we may also call it, the doctrine of the

[1] From *Humanistic Viewpoints in Psychology* by F. T. Severin. Copyright 1965 by McGraw-Hill Book Co. Used with permission of McGraw-Hill Book Co.

3

primary reactivity of the psychophysiological organism. Behavior is response to stimuli coming from outside. This principle of reactivity entails that of *environmentalism* or other-directedness, to 'use Riesman's term. So far as it is not innate or instinctive, behavior is shaped by outside influences that have met the organism in the past: classical conditioning after Pavlov, instrumental conditioning after Skinner, early childhood experience after Freud, secondary reinforcements after more recent theories. Hence training, education and human life in general are essentially response to outside conditions... (pp. 7–8).[2]

There are inherent dangers in the robot model, however. Bertalanffy adds,

It is well to realize both the power and the limits of manipulating psychology and behavioral engineering. If you manipulate a dog according to Pavlov, a cat according to Thorndike, or a rat according to Skinner, you will obtain the results described by these authors. That is, you select, out of their behavior repertoire, such responses as may be controlled by punishment or reward, you *make* the animals into stimulus-response machines or robots. The same, of course, is true of humans. Any well-conducted campaign—say, the last Christmas sale of war toys—is as neat a piece of behavioral experimentation as any in the laboratory. Modern psychology has all tricks to turn human beings into subhuman automata, or into a mob screaming for destruction of a supposed enemy or even of themselves: it is just a question of routine techniques used by any car dealer or television advertiser. However, in so doing, you de-rattisize rats and de-humanize humans (p. 13).[3]

The consequent result is that "in the end, the effects of modern psychotechniques and behavioral engineering amount to *functional decerebralization,* that is, exclusion of higher cerebral centers and mental faculties—almost as efficiently as if these were removed by surgical operation" (p. 16).[4]

Matson, in *The Broken Image* (1964), refers to the "mechanomorphized" view of man, in which conscious experience has been excluded. The title of Matson's book was taken from a warning by Paul Tillich, "Man resists objectification; and if his resistance to it is broken, man himself is broken" (Tillich, 1951, p. 98).

Teilhard de Chardin, in *The Phenomenon of Man* (1959), speaks of mechanized man:

At no previous period of history has mankind been so well equipped nor made

[2] From *Robots, Men and Minds* by Ludwig von Bertalanffy; reprinted with the permission of the publisher. Copyright © 1967 by Ludwig von Bertalanffy.
[3] *Ibid.*
[4] *Ibid.*

such efforts to reduce its multitudes to order. We have "mass movements"—no longer the hordes streaming down from the forests of the north or the steppes of Asia, but "the Million" scientifically assembled. The Million in rank and file on the parade ground; the Million standardised in the factory; the Million motorised —and all this only ending up with Communism and National-Socialism and the most ghastly fetters. So we get the crystal instead of the cell; the ant-hill instead of brotherhood. Instead of the upsurge of consciousness which we expected, it is mechanisation that seems to emerge inevitably from totalisation (p. 256).[5]

DETERMINED MAN

Rogers distinguishes between two trends in psychotherapy, the *objective trend* and the *existential trend* (Rogers, in May, 1961). The objective trend emphasizes the concrete, the operationally defined, the lack of freedom in human behavior. Skinner exemplifies the deterministic viewpoint in the statement, ". . . An analysis which appeals to external variables makes the assumption of an inner originating and determining agent unnecessary" (1953, p. 241).

Psychoanalytic theory also proposes the lack of freedom in human behavior:

Psychoanalytic theory, for example, is strictly deterministic in the sense that behavior is assumed to be lawful and caused. Specific acts and experiences, as well as behavior in general, are assumed to be related causally to antecedent conditions. The view of man which emerges from the theory is essentially mechanistic, for he is seen as a creature who always responds to the present and the future in terms of historical determinants, propelled inexorably by a multiplicity of drives, motives, and impulses from within, in conjunction with the harsh demands of reality from without (Temerlin, in Severin, 1965, p. 69).[6]

ENCAPSULATED MAN

In spite of the phenomenal growth and advancement of his civilization, contemporary man still perceives reality myopically. J. R. Royce (1964) refers to this narrowness of vision as *encapsulation*. He states,

---

[5] From *The Phenomenon of Man* by Pierre Teilhard de Chardin. Copyright 1965 by Editions de Seuil. Copyright © by Wm. Collins Sons & Co. Ltd., London, and Harper & Row, Publishers, Inc., New York.

[6] Severin, *op. cit.*

By encapsulated I mean claiming to have the whole of truth when one has only part of it. By encapsulated I mean looking at life partially and proceeding to make statements concerning the whole of life. And by encapsulated I mean living partially because one's daily activities are based on a worldview or philosophy of life which is meager next to the larger meaning of existence (pp. 2–3).[7]

The problem of encapsulation is one that has plagued man for centuries and, to a degree, is characteristic of the finiteness of man. It is a danger that will always accompany the search for a comprehensive theory of man.

ALIENATED MAN

Kenneth Keniston, in his book *The Uncommitted* (1965), portrays the loneliness of the present age:

Alienation, estrangement, disaffection, anomie, withdrawal, disengagement, separation, noninvolvement, apathy, indifference, and neutralism—all of these terms point to a sense of loss, a growing gap between men and their social world. The drift of our time is away from connection, relation, communion, and dialogue, and our intellectual concerns reflect this conviction. Alienation, once seen as imposed *on* men by an unjust economic system, is increasingly chosen *by* men as their basic stance toward society (p. 3).[8]

Keniston describes four types of alienation: (*a*) "cosmic outcastness"—the loss of connection with a divinely or metaphysically structured universe that "cares" about man; (*b*) "developmental estrangements"—a sense of the loss in individual life of ties and relationships that can never be recreated; (*c*) "historical loss"—a loss due to rapid, worldwide, and chronic social change: and (*d*) "self-estrangement"—a lack of contact between the individual's "conscious self" and his "real self," manifest in a sense of unreality, emptiness, flatness, and boredom.

Alienation in contemporary man is also illustrated in Albert Camus's existential novels *The Stranger* (1954) and *The Fall* (1956). Greening compares Camus's theories of alienation with the theory of authenticity (Greening, in Bugental, 1967).

---

[7] From *The Encapsulated Man* by Joseph R. Royce, copyright © 1964, by Litton Educational Publishing, Inc., by permission of Van Nostrand Reinhold Co.

[8] Reprinted with permission of Harcourt Brace Jovanovich, Inc.

VIOLENT MAN

Violence should be distinguished from aggression in general, of which violence is but one form (Gilula and Daniels, 1969; Gilula, Daniels, and Ochberg, 1969). Violence is manifest in American society in civil riots, campus revolts, and in individual assaults with deadly weapons. For example,

In 1967 firearms caused approximately 21,500 deaths—approximately 7,700 murders, 11,000 suicides, and 2,800 accidental deaths. In addition, there were also about 55,000 cases of aggravated assault by gun and 71,000 cases of armed robbery by gun. Between 1960 and 1967, firearms were used in 96 percent (that is, 394) of 411 murders of police officers. More than 100,000 nonfatal injuries were caused by firearms during 1966. A study in Chicago in which assaults with guns were compared to those with knives shows many more equally serious assaults with knives than with guns; but more of the gun assaults were fatal. Another study convincingly shows that the mere presence of a gun serves as a stimulus to aggression, that is, "The finger pulls the trigger, but the trigger may also be pulling the finger" (Gilula and Daniels, 1969).[9]

On the world scene, universal nuclear annihilation is an ever-present specter of ultimate human violence.

ANXIOUS MAN

May (1967) has traced the historical roots of the anxiety in modern man. He observes,

...when the presuppositions, the unconscious assumptions of values, in a society are generally accepted, the individual can meet threats on the basis of these presuppositions. He then reacts to threats with fear, not anxiety. But when the presuppositions in a society are themselves threatened, the individual has no basis on which to orient himself when he is confronted with a specific threat. Since *the inner citadel of society itself is in a state of confusion and traumatic change during such periods*, the individual has no solid ground on which to meet the specific threats which confront him. The result for the individual is profound disorientation, psychological confusion, and hence chronic or acute panic and anxiety (p. 70).[10]

---

[9] From *Violence and Man's Struggle to Adapt*, Gilula, M. F. and Daniels, D. N., *Science*, Vol. 164, pp. 396–405, 25 April 1969. Copyright 1969 by the American Association for the Advancement of Science.

[10] From *Psychology and the Human Dilemma* by Rollo May, copyright © 1967 by Litton Educational Publishing Inc., by permission of Van Nostrand Reinhold.

Thus the collapse of faith in the traditionally stable values of society is a primary cause of contemporary anxiety.

Tillich defines anxiety as the existential awareness of ultimate nonbeing, the awareness of one's finitude as finitude (1952). He further describes three forms of human anxiety: anxiety of fate and death, anxiety of emptiness and loss of meaning, and anxiety of guilt and condemnation. The first type of anxiety stems from man's awareness of the ultimate termination of mortal existence, as well as the experience of the contingencies of fate, e.g., unforeseen and apparently meaningless disasters. The second form of anxiety relates to "the loss of an ultimate concern, of a meaning which gives meaning to all meanings. This anxiety is aroused by the loss of a spiritual center, of an answer, however symbolic and indirect, to the question of the meaning of existence" (1952, p. 47). Tillich's third type of anxiety is related to human freedom and the anxiety accompanying failure in responsibility.

Man is essentially "finite freedom"; freedom not in the sense of indeterminacy but in the sense of being able to determine himself through decisions in the center of his being. Man, as finite freedom, is free within the contingencies of his finitude. But within these limits he is asked to make of himself what he is supposed to become, to fulfill his destiny. In every act of moral self-affirmation man contributes to the fulfillment of his destiny, to the actualization of what he potentially is (1952, p. 52).[11]

It is the loss of this destiny that gives rise to anxiety.

MEANINGLESS MAN

The loss of significant values, with the consequent meaninglessness of human existence, is adequately described by J. R. Royce in his work *The Encapsulated Man* (1964):

And 20th-century history clearly demonstrates that the so-called rational West has been the source of the greatest devastation and irrationality known to civilized man. Contemporary man, especially Western man, is confused by all this, and he is searching for a new sense of orientation to life. Contemporary man finds himself in a paradoxical predicament. He has more political freedom, more personal freedom from the slavery of hard work, and better health and more material advantages than his predecessors. While, in general, man has never had it so good, the future of mankind has never looked so bad. For the contemporary paradox

[11] From *The Courage to Be* by Paul Tillich, reprinted by permission of Yale University Press.

of the human predicament is that in spite of possessing all the earmarks of happiness, the inner man has rarely been more miserable. The situation can be summed up by saying that contemporary man is suffering from the malady of *meaninglessness*. Modern movements such as existentialism and the revival of interest in religion point rather decisively to the inadequacy of traditional values. And the restless searching which is manifest in the major cultural outlets, such as the arts and science, are indicative of the inability of traditional symbols to carry the weight of a meaningful existence (p. 2, italics added).[12]

Kemp (1967) writes,

We desire meaning but we are not certain what we seek. Only dimly aware of what it is we lack, we look in the wrong places and ask the wrong questions. The answers we receive point to travel, sight-seeing, promotion, position, and possessions. The character of our goals reveals our horizontal living, our immersion in our world of technical reason. If the results are not fully satisfying we assure ourselves that with more knowledge and "research" better solutions will be found.

This attitude and manner of life Tillich called the "horizontal dimension." He finds on every hand examples that illustrate its character. He writes: "Indeed our daily life, in office and home, in cars and airplanes, at parties and conferences, while reading magazines and watching television, while looking at advertisements and hearing radio, are in themselves continuous examples of a life which has lost the dimension of depth. It runs ahead, every moment is filled with something which must be done or seen or said or planned." Such behavior, then, prevents us from asking the meaningful questions, those which would help us to understand ourselves and relate to others with honesty and sincerity (p. 121).[13]

Bertalanffy observes,

Ours is the affluent society, so we read, and we have the highest standard of living ever achieved. We are bombarded with astronomical figures of gross national product—20 billion dollars for the first trip to the moon, 11 billion dollars for packaging wares to make them appetizing to the buyer. But we also read of 100 billion dollars which would be required but is not available for slum clearing; we read that 57 percent of people over age sixty-five live on less than $1,000 a year in cold-water flats, that 10 percent of Americans are functional illiterates. And what is perhaps the most remarkable symptom, economic opulence goes hand in hand with a peak of mental illness, some 50 percent of hospital beds being occupied by mental patients. It goes hand in hand with a continuous increase in

[12] From *The Encapsulated Man* by Joseph R. Royce, copyright © 1964, by Litton Educational Publishing, Inc., by permission of Van Nostrand Reinhold Co.

[13] From C. G. Kemp, *Intangibles in Counseling*, Boston: Houghton Mifflin, 1967.

the rate of crime, especially juvenile delinquency. And, the psychotherapists tell us, besides the classical neuroses caused by stress, tensions, and psychological trauma, a new type of mental sickness has developed for which they have even had to coin a new term—existential neurosis, mental illness arising from the meaninglessness of life, the lack of goals and hopes in a mechanized mass society (Bertalanffy, in Bugental, 1967, p. 336).[14]

May describes modern man's loss of significance:

In a period of transition, when old values are empty and traditional mores no longer viable, the individual experiences a particular difficulty in finding himself in his world. More people experience more poignantly the problem of Willie Loman in *Death of a Salesman*, "He never knew who he was." The basic dilemma, inhering in human consciousness, is part of all psychological experience and present in all historical periods. But in times of radical cultural change, as in sexual mores and religious beliefs, the particular dilemmas which are expressions of the basic human situation become harder to negotiate. To begin with, I pose the question, Is not one of the central problems of modern Western man that he experiences himself as without significance as an individual? . . . My thesis is that the problem of identity in the 1950's has now become, more specifically, the crisis of the loss of the sense of significance. It is possible to lack a sense of identity and still preserve the hope of having influence—"I may not know who I am, but at least I can make them notice me." In our present stage of loss of sense of significance, the feeling tends to be, "Even if I did know who I am, I couldn't make any difference as an individual anyway" (p. 26).[15]

The consequences are severe:

When the individual loses his significance, there occurs a sense of apathy, which is an expression of his state of diminished consciousness. Is not the real danger this surrender of consciousness—the danger that our society will move in the direction of the man who expects the drugs to make him comfortable and the machine not only to satisfy all his needs but, in the form of psychoanalytic mechanisms, to make him happy and able to love as well? When Karl Jaspers talks about the danger of modern man losing his self-consciousness, he is not speaking in hyperbole: we need to take him quite seriously. For this loss is no longer simply a theoretical possibility dreamt up by pychoanalysts or the "morbid existentialist"

[14] From Ludwig von Bertalanffy, "The world of science and the world of value," in James F. T. Bugental, *Challenges of Humanistic Psychology*, New York: McGraw-Hill, copyright 1967. Used with permission of McGraw-Hill Book Co.
[15] May, *op. cit.*

philosophers. This diminution of consciousness, I believe, is central to the deepest form of the loss of the sense of significance (pp. 35–36).[16]

EMERGING MAN

In addition to these formidable images of contemporary man, there is an optimistic interpretation of human nature, one that has long been known in the humanities, but which psychology has only recently rediscovered. It has been designated as the "third force" in psychology, an addition to the movements of behaviorism and psychoanalysis. This new designation

...has since been applied to phenomenological psychology, existential psychology, and humanistic psychology, respectively or collectively. Perhaps this appellation is . . . intended to refer to the distinguishing common feature of the three movements together, [rather] than to any of them alone. This common feature or core seems to be principally the emphasis on man as a person, on his unique subjective problems, and on the use of any methods capable of advancing our knowledge of man; or simply, to cite J.F.T. Bugental, the emphasis on "the functioning and experience of a whole human being." A comparison of the postulates and aims of these movements reveals indeed close parallels between them. The Articles of Association of the American Association for Humanistic Psychology describe humanistic psychology in these words: "Humanistic psychology is primarily an orientation toward the whole of psychology rather than a distinct area or school. It stands for respect for the worth of persons, respect for differences of approach, openmindedness as to acceptable methods, and interest in exploration of new aspects of human behavior. As a 'third force' in contemporary psychology it is concerned with topics having little place in existing theories and systems: e.g., love, creativity, self, growth, organism, basic need-gratification, self-actualization, higher values, being, becoming, spontaneity, play, humor, affection, naturalness, warmth, ego-transcendence, objectivity, autonomy, responsibility, meaning, fair-play, transcendental experience, peak experience, courage, and related concepts" (Misiak and Sexton, 1966, p. 454).

Two very good texts of edited readings reflecting this emerging "third force" are those of Severin (1965) and Bugental (1967).

The concept of man's intrinsic value has been summarized by Bittle (1945):

Some authors, with a facetious turn of mind, speak of man as a worm crawling on a pebble, the earth, as a speck of life floating aimlessly through the immeasurable vastness of the universe. The idea is puerile. As if the greatness of a thing should be measured in terms of physical size and linear dimensions! Man's body

[16] *Ibid.*

stands at the half-way mark between the mass of the infinitesimal electron and the mass of the most ponderous star; he is the *pivotal point of the universe*. Comprising within his organic body subatomic particles, the chief elements, and all that is best in plants and animals, he is the *supreme representative of the universe*. His spiritual soul, with its penetrating intellect and conquering will enables him to pierce the view of phenomena and uncover the hidden essences and laws, so that he is the natural *interpreter of the universe*. One single spiritual concept far outweighs the huge massiveness of an entire world of mere matter. One single spiritual soul has a greater value and a nobler destiny than a million solar systems and a billion galaxies of blindly whirling stars. In the spirituality of his soul, he is the *crown of the universe*. With his feet he is rooted in matter; but his soul reaches out beyond the uttermost boundaries of matter and space (pp. 598–599).[17]

The viewpoint of the present work will be generally a humanistic one, and specifically, a Christian one. Thus far, various images of contemporary man have been presented in summary. The challenge is to discover the image most appropriate to man as he really is. It will be contended here that man himself has fashioned these self-images, and what man has made he can unmake or, better still, he can remake. The intrinsic dignity of man is the key to growth, becoming, and fulfillment, and this perspective of human nature will be examined in the chapters to follow.

[17] From Rev. Celestine Bittle, O.F.M., Cap., *The Whole Man*, New York: Bruce Publishing Co., 1945.

Chapter 2

Evaluations of Human Nature

Since his beginning, man has endlessly explored various paths in quest of the meaning and purpose of his world. The search starts with the childhood question Why? Modern man has achieved great progress in fathoming the secrets of the universe, and the satisfaction of increased technology has been richly rewarding, but only in a materialistic sense. Knowledge of and use of his environment alone are not sufficient; there is still the challenge of finding the purpose for *human* existence.

Ways of pursuing the answer are as diverse as the thinking of those who have accepted the challenge. Although we must give credit to the organizing power of disciplines such as art, history, and the social sciences, there is one classification to which all branches of knowledge are amenable. This classification is the threefold division of science, philosophy, and divine revelation (Table 1). Such a classification has the desirable feature of being

Table 1. Three Approaches in Studying Human Nature

Approach	Method	Instrument	Product
Science	Experimental	Senses	Quantitative data
Philosophy	Rational	Mind	Ideas, concepts, truths
Divine revelation	Theological	Soul (through faith)	Divine precepts

based on the nature of man, in that all human experience is arrived at on a sensory, intellectual, or spiritual level.

SCIENCE

Of the approaches to the study of human nature, the procedure used in science, the experimental method, yields the least disputable data, in that such data are readily observable and can be replicated. This approach, therefore, is the one most widely used in the study of human behavior, and it has settled many armchair disputes.

For example, the U.S. Army had for many years debated the use of the rifle sling as an aid to marksmanship in combat firing. The rifle sling is a strap attached to the rifle for carrying the weapon conveniently. Sometime during the history of weapon usage, the sling was adapted as a supposed aid in steadying the rifle during firing, While one end of the sling was left attached to the weapon, the other was looped tightly around the upper arm of the firer. Many World War II veterans of the European campaign favored the sling as an aid to accurate marksmanship, whereas most veterans of Pacific battles considered it a hindrance during jungle fighting, especially to mobility in dense underbrush.

A series of experiments conducted at the Infantry School at Fort Benning, Georgia (Hammes et al., 1957; McFann, Hammes, and Taylor, 1955), left no doubt that the sling was of little value to the infantry soldier receiving only the prescribed basic rifle marksmanship training. These experiments, first conducted by scientists, then further replicated by Army officials, illustrate the value of the experimental method in settling disputes about human behavior.

Another example of settling arguments by the scientific method is that of research in fallout-shelter occupancy. Despite morbid predictions of psychological and physiological breakdown in groups undergoing long-term isolation and confinement, it has been demonstrated that initially healthy men, women, and children can endure austere confinement conditions on semi-starvation diets for periods as long as two weeks (Hammes Ahearn, and Keith, 1965; Hammes and Osborne, 1965, 1966; Hammes et al., 1965).

PHILOSOPHY

As seen in Table 1, philosophy is an approach applying human intelligence to the study of man. The consequent products, viz., ideas, concepts, and truths, are less readily observable than the quantitative data of science, and are therefore subject to greater dispute. However, the nonquantitative nature of the rational method is not a valid reason for rejecting this approach in the study of man. Even the scientist plays the role of philosopher in his interpretation of quantitative data. The term *rational method* has a unique meaning here, in that it signifies the intelligent analysis and synthesis of behavioral data on the *level of immediate inference*. Such inferences indicate variables that really exist, although they are inaccessible to experimental quantification and verification. Inferred variables can be logically demonstrated, and actually have validity equal to those observable on the sensory level of experimentation.

Confidence in the rational method obviously depends on confidence in the capability of the human mind to attain valid certitude about the existence of things unobserved by the senses. That such confidence is justified will be demonstrated in future chapters. Establishing valid premises and reasoning correctly from them are also essential requisites of the rational method.

DIVINE REVELATION

In identifying the third method of studying man, the term *divine revelation* is preferable to the more inclusive term *religion*. Religion embraces both divinely revealed truth and truths naturally arrived at by the human mind concerning man's relationship to God. Divine revelation, on the other hand, is used here to denote those truths that lie beyond man's capability of discovery and must be communicated to him precisely for that reason. The Trinity of God illustrates a divinely revealed truth, accepted on the basis of faith rather than reason.

What is faith? It is "the substance of things to be hoped for, the evidence of things that appear not," according to St. Paul (Heb. 11:1). It can also be defined as a gift from God, illuminating the mind with a special clarity, moving it to accept what is not understood by reason alone. Faith does not contradict reason, but rather supplements it. Faith is not unreasonable; it lies beyond reason. Faith is not blind; it is enlightenment. Faith rests on divine authority, not human authority. "If we receive the testimony of men, the testimony of God is greater.... He that believeth in the Son of God hath the testimony of God in himself" (1 John 5:9–10). Faith is not possessed by all, but only by those to whom God gives it. And those with faith possess it in degree; hence, greater depth of faith may be found in some persons than in others.

Another example of divinely revealed truth is the Ten Commandments, dictated to man because by his own efforts he would never have arrived at their necessity or their number. "The Lord spoke all these words..." (Exod. 20:1). "... And he wrote them on two tablets of stone, which he delivered unto me" (Deut. 5:22). A further analysis of faith is given in Chapter 15.

EXTREMISTS

The preceding three approaches to studying man and human behavior have well-known advocates: the scientist, the philosopher, and the theologian. There are also overlapping interests (Figure 1). The scientist, after collecting experimental data, adds meaning through theorizing, an expression of the rational method. The philosopher uses his intellect as the chief instrument of study, but will draw on experimental and theological sup-

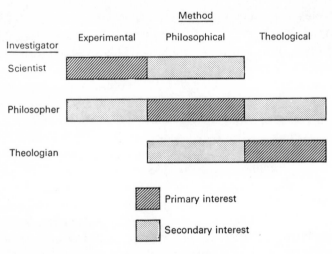

FIG. 1.   Overlapping interests of investigators.

port for his philosophical data. The theologian searches Scripture for the meaning of man's existence, but must also rely on his own rational processes to reconcile apparent contradictions between science and theology. Unfortunately, in all three approaches there are found extremists, individuals who consider their singular approach the only valid way of studying human behavior. The chief offender in psychology is the scientist who repudiates philosophy and theology as valid sources of information concerning the origin, nature, and destiny of man. However, extremism in any of these three areas will produce a distorted and unrealistic portrait of human nature. That such has occurred will be demonstrated in subsequent chapters.

It will be the viewpoint in this text that all three approaches are necessary for attaining a complete and comprehensive analysis of human behavior and man's nature. Each method can be shown to be valid, and each has a contribution for psychological theory.

OPERATIONISM IN PSYCHOLOGY

The full story of operationism and its ancestor, logical positivism, has been well recorded elsewhere (Boring, 1950). A brief summary will suffice here. Positivism refers to data that are basic, observational, preinferential, and undebatable. Such data are attainable only by the experimental method, and consequently, positivism became the "philosophy" of science, early espoused by the so-called Vienna circle consisting of Moritz Schlick, Otto Neurath, Rudolph Carnap, and Philipp Frank. Herbert Feigl introduced logical positivism to P. W. Bridgman, a Harvard professor with the same notion (Bridgman, 1927). The ultimate consequence was the adoption of operationism in American psychology, the forerunner being S. S. Stevens (Stevens, 1939). Operationism can be summarized as (*a*) the reduction of statements about observations to simplest terms, (*b*) admission of only publicly observed data, with private or introspective experience being excluded, (*c*) preference for data on the "other one," the subject observed, rather than on the experimenter, and (*d*) admission of only those propositions whose truth value can be tested, the test to consist of concrete operations. Although Stevens contended that operationism is not a new school of psychology, it would certainly seem that it is. The basic tenets of operationism assume the experimental method to be the only valid procedure. This in itself is a philosophical point of view, as well as one that can be questioned (Wolman, 1960; Donceel, 1965).

THE VALUE OF OPERATIONISM

The primary contribution of operationism is the insistence on observable data and concrete procedures for obtaining it. Certainly, if psychology is to be considered at least partly a science, its methodology should be quantitative as far as possible. But there is a realm of human behavior inaccessible to quantification, which nonetheless deserves the attention of the psychologist. The factors *behind* behavior are more important than is behavior itself. Operationism provides but the first step. Another limitation of operationism is that which is true of the experimental method in general, namely, the inability to yield absolute data. Prediction based on quantitative data is made in terms of probability, not certitude. All scientific data in the last analysis are but probable data, based on a changing reality. Operationism will never yield information of an absolute nature. That such information is possible by other means, however, will be demonstrated in Chapter 3 .

RELATIVISM IN PSYCHOLOGY

Relativism, the position that the mind can only know truth subject to future change, dates back to Greek philosophy. This position was given new impetus in philosophy by William James's 1907 work on pragmatism (1943). Pragmatism demands emphasis on the practical and the utilitarian. The criterion of truth is whether or not it works and is of applied value. Pragmatism rebels against the search for finality in truth, or absolute certitude, because such is considered nonexistent. Pragmatism, in other words, considers truth to be relative and contingent on change. Today's truth is tomorrow's error.

Relativism in contemporary psychology is nicely illustrated in the definition of theory as a cluster of relevant assumptions systematically related to each other and to a set of empirical definitions (Hall and Lindzey, 1957). Theories, therefore, are neither true nor false, only useful. As long as the assumptions of a theory are consistent with one another and with observed data, that theory is considered to be valid.

But are these sufficient criteria for valid theorizing? Consider Mesmer, who interpreted suggestibility in terms of animal magnetism. Sick persons touching certain iron rods were cured, and Mesmer ascribed their healing to magnetism, inherent in the earth and influencing man. However, Ben

Franklin, among others, demonstrated that people whose illness is psychological in nature—for example, hysteria—are really cured through hypnosis or suggestion. Nonetheless, Mesmer's assumptions were consistent and in conformity with observed data.

It would seem, therefore, that inner consistency and outer compatibility with known data are necessary but insufficient conditions for good theory. As a final requisite, theory must give insight into reality and things as they are. Thus, theory must reflect objective truth. A theory of human behavior, if it is to be valid and true, must describe the nature of man as it really is.

The relativist has some insight into the limitation of his position, and he attempts to bolster it by adding a criterion for theory evaluation. This criterion is utility, in terms of verifiability and comprehensiveness, rather than truth or falsity (Hall and Lindzey, 1957). Verifiability is further defined in terms of experimental prediction and testing. But even Mesmer could predict with success his cures, and his explanation was compatible with observed data. Furthermore, the interpretation of utility in experimental terms can be questioned. Does not absolute truth possess utilitarian value?

Relativism therefore reduces psychological theory to human opinion. There can be as many theories as there are psychologists. The criteria of good theory, as set up by relativism and operationism, have indeed led to a plethora of theories in every branch of psychology. Furthermore, the basic assumption of relativism is that psychology must be content to build changing theory upon changing phenomena, and that absolute certitude regarding the nature of man is forever unattainable. That such a fatalistic position is unnecessary will be demonstrated in the next chapter.

LINGUISTIC ANALYSIS

Logical positivism, in its relativistic aspect, has led to the development of an approach to knowledge known as linguistic analysis (Barbour, 1966). Truth is reducible to language, and there are as many languages as there are disciplines of knowledge. Thus science, philosophy, and religion use separate languages, serving a diversity of function. For example, the language of religion is actor-language and that of science is spectator-language. The two are complementary and do not interact. This alternative-languages approach attempts to avoid contradictions. For example, it is meaningless to argue whether or not a behavioral act is free or not free (determined). It is both. From the actor-language point of view, the act is free, and from the spectator-language perspective, it is determined. Similarly, mind and brain are not separate entities, but rather constitute two perspectives (languages) on the one and same set of events.

As attractive as linguistic analysis might appear, it is actually a form of logic-tight compartmentalization. It would indeed be nice if contradictions could be resolved by keeping the contradictory components logically separated, but this approach evades the issue. Reality cannot be hidden under the cloak of semantics. Reality exists prior to language and is not contingent on language. Language should be a means of *describing* reality, not a means of determining its nature. The problems of mind-brain, freedom-determinism, vitalism-mechanism, and so on will be evaluated on the objective evidence available, rather than buried arbitrarily in alternative languages. Thus it will be seen that man is capable of two distinct kinds of behavior, free behavior and determined behavior, and that a particular behavioral act is free *or* determined, not both (Chapter 8). Again, man is composed of mind *and* brain, and each has mutually exclusive properties that reject any identity (Chapter 6). Also, either/or categories will be seen to originate in reality. They are not reducible to mere conventions of language (Chapter 3).

THEORY AND RESEARCH

Behavioral theorists also contend that any theory incapable of generating research is useless (Hall and Lindzey, 1957). Perhaps this is true of behavioral theory, but is is an inappropriate criterion to apply to theory that analyzes what *underlies* behavior. Explanation dealing with essence, nature, or the substrate beneath behavior is concerned with the unobservable, which, though untestable, is nonetheless real. It is not behavior under analysis here, but rather its source. Even though a theory of essence may not generate research, it can be compatible with behavioral theories that do. The Christian interpretation of man presented in this text will be seen to be compatible with research findings on human behavior.

PSYCHOLOGY AS A SCIENCE

In conclusion, it would seem that the adoption of relativism and operationism in psychology, together with the repudiation of philosophical and theological approaches, is consequential to the attempt to restrict psychology to a *scientific* study of behavior. Historically speaking, this premise is the result of the development of the sciences in general, as well as of the influence of Darwinian evolution. However, it should be kept in mind that the restriction of psychology (*a*) to scientific investigation and (*b*) to behavior as the only admissible subject matter represents a philosophical rather than a scientific position. Psychology need not be bound to such a restriction. It will be the position of this text that psychology should not be so bound.

Furthermore, the psychologist need not fear to go beyond the empirical and experimental investigation of behavior. He must only be clearly aware of the threshold between science and philosophy, and that between philosophy and divine revelation. Scientific fact should be clearly distinguished from philosophical fact, and neither should be confused with divine revelation. Indeed, many self-professed behavioral psychologists have unwittingly stumbled into philosophical entanglements by failing to distinguish between experimental data and the theoretical interpretation of them.

Since one truth will not contradict another, there should be no disagreement between experimentally established data regarding human behavior and those truths proposed by the Christian frame of reference. The remainder of this text will attempt to demonstrate this compatibility.

Chapter 3

Absolute and Relative Certitude

It has been noted in the preceding chapter that the rational method of philosophy is necessary for the complete understanding of human behavior. It was also noted that this method is hazardous, in that its product is unobservable on the sensory level and therefore not readily evident. The basic question is whether or not the human mind can attain certitude that is reliable and trustworthy.

This question raises another. What is the nature of certitude, or, more commonly, what is truth? Truth may be defined as conformity between intellect and reality. When the mind grasps reality as it is, truth is attained; any discrepancy between reality and what the mind perceives is error.

RELATIVE CERTITUDE

What kinds of certitude, or truth, or veridicality can the mind know? There are two classes: relative and absolute (Table 2). Relative truth refers to knowledge contingent on a changing reality. The sun is shining today. Recognition of this fact is a relative certitude, since tomorrow it may rain. The experimental method of science yields relative truth of two further classes. The first class concerns change in scientific knowledge as a function

23

Table 2. Classes of Truth or Certitude

Absolute Truth—Unchanging knowledge of unchanging reality
Relative Truth—(1) Knowledge changing with elimination of error
(2) Knowledge changing as reality changes

of continually perfected techniques. For example, twenty years ago the number of known basic elements was different from that known today. What was true then was only partially true.

The second class of scientific truth involves not changing techniques, but changing reality. For example, the arrangement of stars in the Big Dipper will, after the next thousand years, be different. Since the object of knowledge will change, truth based on this object will accordingly be modified.

Furthermore, a basic tenet of the statistical procedures of the experimental method is that quantitative analysis at best yields relative data. The reliability of an obtained difference between two groups of subjects is expressed in terms of probability. No matter how low the probability level, the risk of rejecting chance is always there. For example, the probability level of .001 indicates that there is only one chance in 1,000 that the obtained results are due to chance—but there is still that slight element of chance that can never be eliminated, no matter how precise the statistical procedures. Therefore, all scientific data are couched in terms of probability. Nor do scientists claim more than that for their data. However, some theorists insist further not only that scientific knowledge must come under the jurisdiction of chance, but that all knowledge must be similarly restricted. It would therefore follow that psychological theory true today may not be true in the future, and that interpretations of human behavior and human nature are always subject to change. Operationism, as seen in the previous chapter, takes this position.

ABSOLUTE CERTITUDE

Absolute certitude may be defined as knowledge of a reality that is not subject to change, a reality that is eternal and universal. An example would be knowledge of the existence of God. The criteria of absolute truth are independence of change, time, space, and man, for any of these reduces certitude to a relative position (Table 3).

Can the human mind attain a certitude unshackled by chance and contingency? Can the intellect grasp reality that is unchanging, absolute, and eternal? Specifically, are there such unchanging realities in human behavior and human nature, and can man know them?

Table 3. Criteria of Absolute Truth

Independence of:
  (1) Time—eternally true
  (2) Change—immutably true
  (3) Space—universally true
  (4) Man—discovered, not created, by man

The question of man's capacity to attain absolute certitude has practical as well as theoretical implications. If human knowledge must be restricted to relative truth, man will be forever frustrated in the quest for eternal truth. The human intellect seeks stability in pursuit of knowledge. Will this goal be forever denied? Furthermore, the problem has great singificance for the moral aspects of human behavior. Does God really exist, or is he a myth, an archaic relative certitude? Should man continue to be governed by the Ten Commandments, or are these no longer applicable to contemporary society? Should new mores and morals be adopted—also to be shed by future generations? Will man ever know the true purpose of his existence, or must he be content with contingent explanations having but temporary appeal?

The pessimism and despair of classical existentialism reflect the meaninglessness of a relative system of truth. Deep within the human spirit lies a yearning, not for make-believe truth, but for certitude that brings absolute assurance, promise, and fulfillment (Gleason, 1964).

The basic human need for the security of absolute truth should not, however, be the basis of its validity. Such an assertion would be tantamount to saying, for example, that God exists because man has a compulsive need to posit His existence. The reality of God, or of any absolute truth, should stand on its own merit, to be discovered by man, not created by him.

THE PRINCIPLE OF CONTRADICTION

That the human mind is capable of attaining absolute certitude can be demonstrated.

The first step is to set up two categories of being. The first category can be an item of choice—for example, an ordinary household pet, the *cat*. The second category will consist of *non-* attached to the first category, *non-cat*. Hence, there have been established two classifications, cat and non-cat. The prefix non- means "all things other than."

The second step is to classify all existing objects into one of the two categories. Thus, broken bottles and toothpicks are things other than cats and fall appropriately into the non-cat class. Lions, tigers, and tomcats would be included under cat, if we defined the term to embrace all members of the cat family. A few moments' reflection will indicate that all existing things can be grouped under one heading or the other, simply because everything is either a cat or something other than a cat.

How about a zoril? Where would it be classified? After the object is identified, it would be clear that a zoril would be included in the non-cat group, since a zoril is a Southern African weasel. Notice that by its nature it belongs in that group, in spite of our initial ignorance of what it was and our consequent inability to classify it. The point is clear—all things existing will be either cats or things other than cats. Similarly, all things existing will be pencils or things other than pencils, people or things other than people and so on. Thus, any object can constitute a category, and as long as the second category is all things other than the first, then everything will fall into one or the other division. Nor can there be a third category "between" these two. Why not? Simply because the two catgories are mutually exclusive.

Suppose, it may be suggested, the two categories were *black* and *white*. Where would *gray* be placed? The difficulty is resolved when it is realized that black and white are not mutually exclusive categories. Black and non-black, or white and non-white should be the divisions established. All other colors, even gray, can then be assigned. Again, it is sometimes pointed out that between the categories of *all* and *nothing* there is the third category of *some*. However, all and nothing are not mutually exclusive. Mutual exclusion would require such classifications as all and non-all, or nothing and non-nothing. In the first instance, *some* would be included in non-all, and in the second instance, *some* would fall under non-nothing. (It should be obvious that, in the second instance, *all* would also be included under non-nothing.)

A further question—does not the classification depend on identification or definition of the categories? Might there not be an unknown object in the universe incapable of classification? By way of answer, let it be assumed that there is such an object. Since the nature of this entity is unknown, it can be referred to as X, the symbol for an unknown quantity. Now, is it not true that everything existing is *either* X or non-X (something other than X)? Of course.

The setting-up of two mutually exclusive categories is independent of language, semantics, or definition. It is a system based on the nature of things, not a fabrication of speech. This principle is referred to in philosophy as the Princip'e of Contradiction, the Principle of the Excluded Middle, or the Principle of Identity (Bittle, 1936).

A last question—might it be possible someday to discover a third category in between, so to speak, the two that are mutually exclusive? The two possible answers to the question are, It *is* possible that someday a third category will be found, and, It is *not* possible that someday a third category will be found. That is, the two answers refer to a *possibility* and a *non-possibility*. Is there a third answer lying between these two? Clearly not, because the two answers are mutually exclusive. Therefore, it is evident that the existence of any third alternative between two mutually exclusive categories is impossible. Ever discovering in the future an additional alternative between two that are mutually exclusive is consequently seen to be impossible.

SELF-EVIDENCE AND PROOF

But can a principle be used to prove itself? Is this not a vicious circle? The answer is simple. No principle can be used to prove itself. Neither can the Principle of Contradiction be used in such a circular manner. The presentation just given is not to be considered a proof, but rather a *demonstration*.* In other words, the Principle of Contradiction is *self-evident*. It cannot be proved, but only exposed. Whether or not it is accepted depends on the clarity with which the reader grasps the self-evidence contained therein.

The reason this principle cannot be proved is the nature of proof. Something is proved on the basis of previously validated data. For example, if John is taller than George, and George is taller than Henry, then John can be proved to be taller than Henry. If a quarter buys more than a dime, and a dime more than a nickel, then it can be proved that a quarter is worth more

---

* Although Bittle (1936) equates *demonstration* with *proof*, these terms are used differently in this text.

than a nickel. In other words, a proof is a conclusion drawn from two valid premises.

Why cannot the Principle of Contradiction be "proved" in this manner? Precisely because it precedes all premises, underlies all data, preexists all other existent data. There is nothing logically prior to this principle from which the principle can be drawn. Even the alternatives of the possibility and impossibility of prior premises are described by the action of the principle.

Therefore, the Principle of Contradiction is considered to be a self-evident truth, with its own clarity of communication. It cannot be proved, only demonstrated. This characteristic, however, should not be construed as a limitation. For example, one cannot prove one's own existence, as the proof presupposes one's existence in the first place. Yet, because one cannot prove one exists, does this lessen the fact that one *does* exist? Of course not. One's existence is another self-evident fact.

AN ABSOLUTE TRUTH

Earlier, the criteria of absolute certitude were established. Absolute truth must reflect a reality independent of time, change, space, and man. Does the Principle of Contradiction meet these requirements?

First, is it independent of time? Consider any moment of the past, e.g., 1,000,000 B.C. Was the principle valid at that time? The two possible answers are, It *was* valid then, and, It was *not* valid then. These possibilities of valid and non-valid are mutually exclusive and the only alternatives possible. Since they describe the only two possible situations *at 1,000,000 B.C.*, it follows that the Principle of Contradiction is *applicable*, and therefore valid, at this point in the past. And so it is for any point in the past. Likewise, the principle can be extended to apply to a similar instance that would exist at any moment in the future. For example, the principle will be valid or not valid at A.D. 3,000,000. There is no third possibility. In describing the only two possible alternatives at any moment of time in the future, the principle must be valid for any moment of the future. Therefore, the Principle of Contradiction can be shown to be true for any moment of the past, as well as for any moment of the future. It is independent of time—that is, it is eternal.

Is this principle independent of change? Independence of time necessarily embraces independence of change. A precept that is eternally true is not subject to change. The Principle of Contradiction, being eternally true, will never change.

Is the principle independent of space, i.e., is it true anywhere in the universe? The question could be posed, Is the Principle of Contradiction valid on the planet Mars? The only two possible answers are, It *is* valid on Mars, and, It is *not* valid on Mars. There is no third alternative answer to this question. Since the principle describes a situation on Mars, it must be applicable to, and therefore valid on, Mars. Hence, this principle is independent of space, or universally true.

Is the principle independent of man? Did the human mind invent it—or discover it? Obviously, if the principle is eternally true, it is independent of temporal man. Man has discovered, not created, the reality of absolute certitude.

The demonstration of the human capability for attaining absolute certitude has great significance and pragmatic value for psychology. Human reason, or the method of immediate inference, when used rightly, is vindicated as a valid source of knowledge concerning human behavior and human nature. There is no necessity, then, to restrict intellectual analysis by the fetters of contingency. Relative truth is of value, but absolute truth is of far greater worth. The psychologist, therefore, has the right to seek such truths in the formulations of the origin, nature, purpose, and destiny of man.

OBJECTIONS TO THE ATTAINMENT OF ABSOLUTE TRUTH

A final question, one undoubtedly in the mind of the reader—why is this demonstration not accepted by all scientists, philosophers, and psychologists? There are many reasons why truth is rejected (Table 4). A primary reason is the assumption that because all things *can* be doubted, they *must* be doubted, a position known as universal skepticism. The validity of the Principle of Contradiction *can* be doubted. But is such a doubt reasonable?

Table 4. Objections to the Attainment of Absolute Truth

(1)	Universal skepticism—compulsion to doubt all certitude
(2)	Assumption of science—absolute truth unattainable
(3)	Training bias—suspicion of intangible data
(4)	Ignorance—other alternatives possible
(5)	Agnosticism—assent withheld
(6)	Relativism—absolute truth impossible

The crux of the issue is the difference between reasonable and unreasonable doubt. One can doubt one's existence, if one wishes. But is this reasonable? Obviously not, because in order to doubt, one must first exist. Just because the human mind *can* doubt all truth, it does not follow that such capability of universal doubt demands acceptance. The only fact demonstrated by such a capability is that the human mind can entertain two kinds of skepticism, reasonable and unreasonable. To doubt one's own existence and to doubt absolute certitude such as the Principle of Contradiction exemplify unreasonable doubting. Such doubts should not be compulsive, and are unworthy of keeping.

Interestingly, the Principle of Contradiction can be applied to those who doubt it. The individual can be described as doubting or not doubting, agreeing or not agreeing, arguing or not arguing, as being convinced or not convinced, and so on.

Another reason for rejecting truth is the unwitting use of invalid premises. Much psychological theory stems from basic assumptions that are not clearly delineated and are in error. An example is the assumption that the experimental method is the only valid approach to analyzing human behavior, and that all truth is reduced to mere probability. Such a position is gratuitous and, as will be seen, produces a distorted interpretation of man.

The logical positivists and linguistic analysts (Ayer, 1946; Feigl and Sellars, 1949) would reject the absolute nature of the Principle of Contradiction on the contention that all propositions and truths are functions of subjective language, rather than being rooted in objective reality. Furthermore, they would contend that statements incapable of being verified by sense-data are meaningless or tautological. However, it has been noted that even those who disagree with the validity of the Principle of Contradiction are subject to its description, i.e., agreeing or not-agreeing. It has also been observed that the basis of the Principle of Contradiction is prior to language, and independent of language. Any object would be X or non-X by its very objective nature. Reality does not depend on language description. Furthermore, such critics as Barbour (1966) point out that the demands of logical positivists and linguistic analysts, e.g., verification in terms of sense-data alone, are themselves arbitrary conventions, gratuitously assumed, and in no manner absolute, necessary, or compulsive. If one wishes to set up relativistic assumptions, that is one's prerogative, but in no instance is one justified in condemning those who prefer to accept the evidence for absolute certitude.

Indoctrination bias can cloud acceptance of truth. Behaviorally trained psychologists are taught to be suspicious of intangible data, erroneously associated with superstitious mysticism and loose thinking. Any abuse of the rational method of philosophy is no reason to reject its proper and correct use. That such use can lead to valid information has been demonstrated.

Finally, a very subtle criticism of absolute truth is the charge that it is accepted because the contrary is inconceivable. Therefore, ignorance of any alternative is the actual reason for accepting absolute certitude! This contention, of course, is false. Ignorance can never be the basis of any certitude. It has been demonstrated that the self-evidence of the Principle of Contradiction communicates its own clarity of certitude, and impresses intelligence in a positive, rather than a negative, manner. Indeed, to accept any alternative to absolute truth is to accept error.

AN OPEN MIND

Another objection to the capability of the mind to attain absolute certitude is that of agnosticism. An agnostic is a "not-knower," a person who suspends final judgment because of the possibility of error. Agnosticism, however, is a double-edged sword. While the agnostic will never be caught wrong, he will also never be caught right. He really asserts nothing, and therefore cannot take a positive position in any state of affairs. To do so, he must leave his agnostic perch. However, even self professed agnostics can be found in the inconsistent position of having quite a bit to say concerning what is correct and incorrect about human behavior.

A viewpoint akin to agnosticism is that of relativism. According to this position, there is no absolute frame of reference or standard against which truth can be measured. This view has been previously discussed in relation to operationism. The fundamental error of relativism is the basic axiom that all things are relative. Such a statement is self-contradictory, in that it is set down as an absolute certitude. It is absurd to state *absolutely* that *all* things are *relative*. The relativist is logically reduced to the position of the agnostic.

When, then, is it advisable to keep an "open mind"? Only in areas where relative truth exists—for example, in the world of science. The physical universe is constantly changing, and true observations must change accordingly. An open mind is essential here. However, in the realm of absolute truth, an open mind is disastrous. The only alternative to absolute truth is error, and to open the mind to error is unreasonable. Furthermore, simply because it is possible to keep one's mind open, it does not follow that this is always a necessary position, just as we have seen that there should be no compulsion to doubt everything simply because we have that ability.

There should be a clear distinction between absolute truth and absolute knowledge, the latter term referring to knowledge of all truth, both absolute and relative. Obviously, no human mind is capable of absolute knowledge, since it is the basic nature of man to learn, and then only to a limited degree. However, the fact that human intelligence can grasp absolute certitude at all is a marvelous capability. Several absolute truths are accessible to man, sufficient in number to reveal the purpose of his existence and the destiny that awaits him. These truths will be discussed in chapters to follow.

It should also be noted that although absolute truth will never change, man's perception, appreciation, and interpretation of absolute truth will. In the evolution of human consciousness, man will inevitably attain a deeper insight into the wealth and significance of absolute truth, and he will accordingly shape his future universe (Teilhard de Chardin, 1959, 1965).

Chapter 4

Causality, Intervening Variables, and Hypothetical Constructs

Causes are intangible and nonquantitative explanations, and as such are unseen and unobservable. Unless a variable is quantifiable in physical terms, the contemporary behavioral psychologist has little interest in it, and therefore little use for factors such as causes. This attitude stems from the influence of operationism in psychology.

An ingenious substitute for cause-effect relationships has been adopted in psychological investigation: the statistical concept of correlation. Correlation coefficients indicate the degree to which variation in one variable accompanies variation in another. They range in value from .00 to $\pm$ 1.00. For example, the greater the number of hours a laboratory rat is deprived of food, the faster it will run to obtain food in a goal box. There will be a high correlation between the two variables, hours of food deprivation and speed of running. In an example of human behavior, the number of study hours and school grades are correlated. In neither instance, however, does the behavioral psychologist speak of hunger as the "cause" of running speed (an "effect") or of study time as the "cause" of better grades. The behavioral scientist believes behavior can be adequately observed and predicted in terms of functional correlational statistics, with no necessity to posit unseen cause-effect relationships.

It is the viewpoint in this text that quantitative analysis of data-gathering is obviously valuable on the behavioral level, but leaves unanswered fundamental questions about what occurs prior to and underneath behavior, i.e., what happens inside the animal or inside man, as the case may be. Only the analysis of cause-effect relationships will yield an interpretive synthesis of isolated quantitative behavioral data, and this evaluation can be accomplished only by use of the rational method, the method of immediate inference.

TYPES OF CAUSALITY

Aristotle resolved causality into four types (Bittle, 1939, 1941). By way of example, consider Michelangelo's statue of David. First, the sculptor himself, necessary for this production, can be designated as the *efficient cause*. Secondly, marble was an essential item and can be termed the *material cause*. Thirdly, the sculpturing process itself was required: it can be referred to as the *formal cause*. A final requisite for the statue was its purpose, and this can be called the *final cause*. Without any one of these four causes, the statue of David would never have been produced.

In simpler language, the efficient cause is the *who* or *by which* something is done, the material cause is the *what* or *out of which* something is done, the formal cause is the *how* or *through which* something is done, and the final cause is the *why* or *for which* something is done (Table 5). All four causes enter into the production of an effect.

Table 5. Types of Causality

Cause	Action Toward Effect
Efficient	Who, or by which
Material	What, or out of which
Formal	How, or through which
Final	Why, or for which

IMMEDIATE INFERENCE

The experimental method of science does not reveal causal relationships, but rather provides discrete data. These data, to be meaningful, must be evaluated by the rational method of philosophy. The rational method has been defined here as use of the level of immediate inference. Hunger as the motivating factor for the rat's running speed would be an inferred variable. Unseen and unobservable, this variable nevertheless appears justified by inference, inference that is grounded in experimental and empirical data.

Causes, then, are inferred variables. As David Hume rightly contended (T.V. Moore, 1939), the cause-effect relationship between cue ball and billiard ball is not sensorially perceived. The eye merely records a succession of events—a cue ball rolling across the table and striking a billiard ball, which then begins to move. To conclude that the cue ball *caused* motion (effect) in the billiard ball is an inference made by the human mind in the analysis of observed data. To reject this reasonable inference is to doubt the capability of the human intellect to yield facts as valid as those recorded by the senses. This David Hume did, and embraced universal skepticism as his philosophical position. It is the position in this text, however, that immediate inference from quantitatively observed data is a sound and valid procedure, based on vindication of the capability of human intelligence, as demonstrated in the previous chapter.

Kant, the idealist, attempted to ascribe causality to a projection of mind only, instead of acknowledging external reality as the source and basis of evidence for causal relationships. The error of Kant's position, that of idealism, will be discussed in Chapter 5.

Additional evidence that causality is a valid inference lies in the distinction experienced between chance and non-chance (cause). Although chance can be defined as the accumulative interaction among unknown causes, the human mind nevertheless discerns the difference between causes acting in an orderly manner and those acting haphazardly (chance).

CAUSALITY IN PSYCHOLOGICAL THEORY

The fourfold division of causality has profound relevance to psychological theory. In the following chapter on personality theory, formal causality will be seen as having played an important role in the history of the mind-body problem, and also as being a vital component of a Christian interpretation of personality. Causality is again important in proving the distinction between mind and brain (Chapter 6), in the evaluation of motivation (Chapter 7), and in the debate on the reality of God (Chapter 12).

INTERVENING VARIABLES AND HYPOTHETICAL CONSTRUCTS

It has been noted that behavioral psychologists prefer explanation of behavior in terms of correlational or functional relationships, rather than in terms of cause-effect relationships. The speed of the rat solving a maze problem can be plotted as a function of the number of hours of food deprivation, or perhaps as a function of shock intensity levels or of some other variable. Ruling out cause-effect relationships, however, is a logical corollary for those who assume the experimental method to be the only valid approach in studying animal or human behavior.

Nevertheless, even the behavioral psychologist has been compelled to consider the possibility of unseen variables *inside* the organism which may account for initiation of behavior subsequently observable. But how can we speak of such variables undetectable by the experimental method? One solution was the invention of the term *hypothetical construct* (MacCorquodale and Meehl, 1948). It was, so to speak, a way of eating one's cake and having it too. The use of the hypothetical construct enables the behavioral psychologist to use terms such as memory, mind, and motive without being inconsistent with his theoretical position of the denial of unseen causal variables. A hypothetical construct is defined as nonexistent, but useful in tying together stimulus-response relationships. The terms *intervening variable* and *logical construct* have also been fashionable (Meissner, 1960; Jessor, 1958). These terms have been quite confused in contemporary psychological theorizing. Investigators do not agree on their definitions, some writers using the terms synonymously and others distinguishing their meanings.

This text will consider the hypothetical construct and the intervening variable to be different concepts (Table 6). Here, *intervening variable* will

Table 6. Classes of Unobservable Variables

Variable	Nature
Intervening variable	Exists as a psychological entity, e.g., mind, or as a physiological entity, e.g., hunger drive
Hypothetical construct	Existence still questioned, e.g., ESP

refer to a variable that exists, but is undetectable by the experimental method and unobserved by the senses. Its existence is arrived at on the level of immediate inference, by use of the rational method of analysis. An example of an intervening variable is the mind, the source of intellectual activity (Chapter 6). *Hypothetical construct*, on the other hand, will denote variables the existence of which is still questioned by psychologists. An example would be extrasensory perception (ESP), such as telepathy (mind communication) or clairvoyance (mind communicating with object, e.g., reading cards). This facility, apparently possessed by few persons and seemingly not always under voluntary control, is still under experimental investigation. While ESP *behavior* is admissible, it is still not clear whether or not the intervening variable underlying this behavior is a human capability above and beyond those presently catalogued, or one reducible to them.

PART I   SUGGESTED READINGS

Abbott, W., Gilbert, A., Hunt, R., and Swaim, J. *The Bible reader: An interfaith interpretation.* New York: Bruce, 1969. Preface, "What is the Bible?"

Adler, M. J. *The conditions of philosophy.* New York: Dell (Delta paperback), 1965. Ch. 2. "The Five Conditions of Philosophy."

Barbour, I. G. *Issues in science and religion.* Englewood Cliffs: Prentice-Hall, 1966. Ch. 6. "The Methods of Science"; Ch. 9. "The Languages of Science and Religion."

Barrett, W. *Irrational man: A study in existential philosophy.* New York: Doubleday (paperback), 1958. Part I. "The Present Age."

Bertalanffy, L. von, *Robots, men, and minds: Psychology in the modern world.* New York: Braziller, 1967. Part I. "Toward a New Image of Man."

Bertalanffy, L. von, *General systems theory: Essays on its foundation and development.* New York: Braziller, 1968. Ch. 8. "The System Concept in the Sciences of Man."

Bittle, C. N. *Reality and the mind: Epistemology.* Milwaukee: Bruce, 1936. Ch. 5. "The Primary Truths": Ch. 15. "The Truth Value of Necessary Judgments"; Ch. 16. "The Criteria of Truth."

Bittle, C. N. *The science of correct thinking: Logic.* Milwaukee: Bruce, 1950. Ch. 6. "Nature of Judgment and Proposition": Ch. 7. "General Types of Propositions."

Boring, E. G. *A history of experimental psychology* (2d Ed.). New York: Appleton-Century-Crofts, 1950. Ch. 24. "Behavioristics."

Bube, R. (Ed.) *The encounter between Christianity and science.* Grand Rapids: Eerdmans, 1968. Preface (Bube); Ch. 1. "The Nature of Science" (Bube); Ch. 9. "Psychology" (Lindquist).

Bugental, J. F. T. *Challenges of humanistic psychology.* New York: McGraw-Hill, 1967. Ch. 1. "The Challenge That Is Man" (Bugental); Ch. 3. "Metaphoric Knowledge and Humanistic Psychology" (Royce); Ch. 16. "The Humanistic Psychology of Teilhard de Chardin" (Severin).

Cole, W. G. *The restless Quest of modern man.* New York: Oxford University Press, 1966. Ch. 1. "The Age of Meaninglessness"; Ch. 3. "The Restless Quest."

Coulson, C. A. *Science and Christian belief.* Chapel Hill: University of North Carolina Press, 1955. Ch. 1. "The Challenge of Scientific Thinking"; Ch. 2. "Scientific Method."

Hall, C. S., and Lindzey, G. *Theories of personality.* New York: Wiley, 1957. Ch. 1. "The Nature of Personality Theory."

Lawrence, N., and O'Connor, D. *Readings in existential phenomenology.* Englewood Cliffs: Prentice-Hall, 1967. Ch. 18. "Phenomenologies and Psychologies."

Marx, M. H., and Hillix, W. A. *Systems and theories in psychology.* New York: McGraw-Hill, 1963. Part I. "Psychology as a Science."

Maslow, A. H. *The psychology of science: A reconnaissance.* New York: Harper & Row, 1966. Ch. 1. "Mechanistic and Humanistic Science"; Ch. 12. "Value-Free Science?"

Matson, F. W. *The broken image: Man, science, and society.* New York: Braziller, 1964. Ch. 2. "The Alienated Machine: Psychology as the Science of Behavior."

May, R. (Ed.) *Existential psychology.* New York: Random House, 1961. Ch. 1. "The Emergence of Existential Psychology" (May); Ch. 2. "Existential Psychology: What's in It for Us?" (Maslow); Ch. 5. "Two Divergent Trends" (Rogers).

May, R. *Psychology and the human dilemma.* Princeton: Van Nostrand, 1967. Part I. "Our Contemporary Situation."

May, R., Angel, E., and Ellenberger, H. F. (Eds.) *Existence.* New York: Simon & Shuster, 1967. Ch. 1. "The Origins and Significance of the Existential Movement in Psychology."

Misiak, H., and Sexton, V. S. *History of psychology: An overview.* New York: Grune & Stratton, 1966. Ch. 21. "Phenomenological Psychology"; Ch. 22. "Existentialism and Psychology."

Raughley, R. *New frontiers of Christianity.* New York: Association Press, 1962. "The Arts" (Elmen); "Philosophy" (Schilpp); "Theology" (Hazelton).

Royce, J. E. *Man and meaning.* New York: McGraw-Hill, 1969. Part I. "Man in the World."

Royce, J. R. *The encapsulated man: An interdisciplinary essay on the search for meaning.* Princeton: Van Nostrand, 1964. Part I. "The Dilemma."

Royce, J. R. (Ed.) *Psychology and the symbol.* New York: Random House, 1965.

Ch. 1. "Psychology at the Crossroads between the Sciences and the Humanities" (Royce).

Rychlak, J. *A philosophy of science for personality theory.* Boston: Houghton Mifflin, 1968. Ch. 5. "The Meanings of Lawfulness and Determinism in Modern Science"; Ch. 9. "Dialectical vs. Demonstrative Reasoning in the History of Western Thought."

Severin, F. T. *Humanistic viewpoints in psychology.* New York: McGraw-Hill, 1965. Introd., Part I. "The Whole Is Greater than the Part" (Severin); Ch. 1. "Humanistic Psychology: A New Breakthrough" (Bugental); Ch. 13. "Persons or Science?" (Rogers); Ch. 30. "The Humanities in an Age of Science" (Harman); Ch. 32. "Psychology: Becoming and Unbecoming" (Turner); Ch. 38. "The Place of the Person in the New World of the Behavioral Sciences" (Rogers).

Shapley, H. *Science ponders religion.* New York: Appleton-Century-Crofts, 1960. Ch. 5. "Notes on the Religious Orientation of Scientists" (Holton); Ch. 15. "Faith and the Teaching of Science" (Kemble); Ch. 16. "Darwin and Religion" (Greene); Ch. 18. "Science, Faith, and Human Nature" (Herrick).

Sutich, A., and Vich, M. (Eds.) *Readings in humanistic psychology.* New York: Free Press, 1969. "Introduction."

Turner, M. B. *Philosophy and the science of behavior.* New York: Appleton-Century-Crofts, 1965. Ch. 8. "The Language of Psychology."

Van Kaam, A. *Existential foundations of psychology.* Pittsburgh: Duquesne Univer. Press (Doubleday paperback), 1969. Ch. 1. "The Nature and Meaning of Science"; Ch. 4. "Differential Theoretical Modes of Existence in Pyschology"; Ch. 12. "Existential and Humanistic Psychology."

Wolman, B. *Contemporary theories and systems in psychology.* New York: Harper & Row, 1960. Ch. 14. "The Scientific Method."

PART II

HUMAN NATURE

Now that approaches to studying man and the validity of human certitude have been established, the next step is to apply these in the examination of human behavior and human nature. Chapter 5 presents an historic survey of personality theory in terms of a philosophical classification, with a proposed Christian interpretation. The vitalism-mechanism controversy is discussed, as well as the relevance of evolution to theory of man's origin.

In Chapter 6 the nature of the human mind and its conceptual process are examined, with comment on the Christian insight into the intrinsic value of human dignity. The dynamic aspects of man are presented in Chapter 7 in the discussion of drive and goal-direction, a discussion that includes an introductory evaluation of man's ultimate life-goal. Finally, in Chapter 8 the relationship of motivated behavior to determinism and freedom is examined in an analysis of ten theories of determinism.

Chapter 5

Human Personality

Since the era of Greek philosophies of personality, the pendulum of thought on this subject has swung between two extremes. The poles of the controversy over the nature of man are *monism* and *dualism*. Simply speaking, monism means "one-ness" and dualism means "two-ness." Is man matter only or spirit only (monism), or is he composed of matter *and* spirit (dualism)? The various classes of personality theory are presented in Table 7.

NATURAL DUALISM AND FORMAL CAUSALITY

As a prefacing remark, it should be noted that some psychologists have contrasted Aristotelian and Galilean modes of thought (Lewin, 1935; Atkinson, 1964), with Aristotle emerging somewhat the worse for wear. However, this judgment is perhaps too sweeping. Although Aristotle's natural physics needs updating, his logical observations on human nature are still valid. His natural dualism has been unfortunately omitted in the majority of psychology texts dealing with this interpretation of man, e.g., Marx and Hillix (1963) and Koch (1959, 1963).

The Christian concept of man's nature is dualistic, patterned after Aris-

Table 7.   Classes of Personality Theory

Theory		Advocates
Dualism	Natural	Aristotle Christian psychology

	Unnatural	Plato
		Descartes
		Psychophysical parallelism of
		    Leibnitz, Malebranche,
		    and Geulincx

Monism	Idealism	Berkeley, Kant, Hegel
	Materialism	Locke, Hume, Hobbes, Haeckel, Comte, Mill Contemporary behavioral psychology and mechanism

totle's analysis. That is, man is composed of both matter (body) and spirit (mind, soul). The relationship is understood in terms of *formal causality*. (Types of causality are defined in Chapter 4.)

Matter is the same in all beings, e.g., chalk, air, skin. If the ear, for example, were dissected to the ultimate subatomic constituents, the electrons isolated would be no different, as electrons, than those existing in glass or wood. Electrons as such are identical. It is obvious, however, that beings differ. If not in their basic material ingredients, then how? Aristotle postulated the difference among existing entities to lie not in matter but in what he termed *form*. The electrons and other subatomic particles are formed or organized differently in different things, giving rise to the multiplicity of beings. Thus, the common element of matter is identical in things, but each thing has a form that makes it what it is. Hence, wood has a form that structures matter into wood, grass has form that determines matter to be grass, and man has a form that gives matter human nature. In summary, form *determines* matter, combining with it to make different substances. (Actually, Aristotle, and later St. Thomas Aquinas, used the terms *primary matter* and *substantial form*. The author, however, prefers the simpler terminology of *matter* and *form*.) In living things, the form can be referred to as the life principle, or vital principle, which vivifies matter, gives it life (Bittle, 1945; Donceel, 1965a, J. E. Royce, 1961).

In the natural order of existence, matter and form are never perceived as separate, but are always seen together, their union forming one substance or one nature. Thus, the term *natural dualism*. Matter and form are never found apart in the natural order—that is, there are no forms floating about apart from matter, and matter is never found without some form. The two variables, even though distinct, are not separated in the natural order. Therefore, man is a composite of matter (body) and form (vital principle). At death, an unnatural state, this form (vital principle) becomes separated from matter (body), which is the reason the dead body is referred to as a corpse, and not as a man. The disembodied vital principle, soul, or spirit, is not a complete person. Hence the reasonableness of the Christian concept of the resurrection of the body, wherein body and soul are once again united to form a complete person, a complete substance, a complete human nature.

Furthermore, the two co-principles of matter and form are mutually irreducible; that is, both are needed, and one alone cannot account for the nature of existing things (Bittle, 1941). They are referred to as *substantial* principles, since together they form a substance.

LOGICAL AND ONTOLOGICAL PRINCIPLES

A distinction should be made between principles that inhere in reality and those fabricated by the human mind (Table 8). A principle of grammar or language, for example, is a product of the mind. Man created such principles, and they have existence only in the mind, i.e., they are not found

Table 8.   Classes of Principles

Principle	Nature
Ontological	Inheres in extra-mental reality, e.g., the principle of gravity
Logical	Fashioned by the mind, e.g., rules of a game

apart from the mind in outside reality. Rules of a game are also invented principles. Principles such as these can be called *logical principles*. On the other hand, there are laws in the physical order that exist apart from the mind, e.g., gravity. The principle of gravity is rooted in extramental reality and was discovered by the human mind, not invented by it. Principles that inhere in the outside world, therefore, are distinct from those humanly created and can be referred to as *ontological principles*.

Matter and form, because they inhere in the very nature of existent beings, are ontological principles. They are causes as well. In the production of human nature, the body (matter), like the marble of Michelangelo's

"David," can be referred to as the *material cause*, and the vital principle (form) as the *formal cause*. Since the vital principle vivifies matter, determines matter to be alive, and is therefore superior to matter, the relationship between vital principle and body is referred to as *formal causality*. The composite, man, would be considered the *efficient cause* of human behavior.

In summary, the distinction between matter and form rests on the observation that since materially all things are identical, there remains the need to account for multiplicity and differentiation. The existence of form as determining matter is a conclusion based on the level of immediate inference. The reasonableness of natural dualism will again be demonstrated in a later discussion of the vital principle and of the distinction between mind and brain.

One final note—natural dualism describes the relationship between the life principle and the body, but does not attempt to explain how the relationship is established. In other words, formal causality is a reasonable explanation of the dual nature of man, but *how* form determines matter is still unknown, not only in man but in all existing things. Does ignorance of the relationship necessitate rejection of this theory? Certainly not. The nature of gravity, electricity, and even life itself is only partially known, yet no one rejects the existence of these realities. One can accept formal causality as a reasonable interpretation of man's makeup, even though the nature of the relationships involved awaits explanation.

UNNATURAL DUALISM

René Descartes (1596–1650), considered by some writers to have marked the beginning of modern psychology and modern philosophy (Boring, 1950), rejected the concept of formal causality, possibly through a misunderstanding of this theory (T.V. Moore, 1939). Instead of considering the source of thought to be the mind (form) and the basis of the body to be matter, Descartes redefined mind as *thought* and the body as *extension*. Thus, the substantial principles of matter and form were replaced by the *actions* proceeding from these principles. The repercussion of Descartes's redefinitions of mind and body has echoed down to the present in both the history of philosophy and the history of science. In physics, for example, matter has become equated with energy, rather than considered as the source of energy, a position held by those favoring the explanation of formal causality.

In philosophy, the effects have been even more complicated. The rejection of substance and the substitution of activity created two factors or processes in man and the consequent problem of an interaction. By analogy there resulted the task of putting Humpty Dumpty together again. The Cartesian concept of two separate processes, thought (mind) and extension (body), became known as *unnatural dualism*.

How, then, do these separate processes exist harmoniously in human nature? One response was the concept of *psychophysical parallelism*, proposed in various forms by Gottfried von Leibnitz (1646–1716), Nicolas de Malebranche (1638–1715), and Arnold Geulincx (1625–1669). In this view, briefly, mind and body never interact, but rather parallel each other so as to give the impression of unity, like two clocks set to the same hour.

MONISM

The other response to the Cartesian dilemma was to consider the mind-body relationship a pseudo-problem. This response maintained that human nature actually consists of one constituent alone (monism). One group of philosophers contended man was pure mind (idealism), and the other group maintained he was pure matter (materialism). Idealism was represented by philosophers such as George Berkeley (1685–1753), Immanuel Kant (1724–1804), and Georg Hegel (1770–1831), while the materialist camp was occupied by David Hume (1711–1776), Thomas Hobbes (1588–1679), Ernst Haeckel (1834–1919), and Auguste Comte (1798–1857). Materialism dates back to the Greek philosophers Democritus and Empedocles (both fifth century, B.C.) and is the basis for mechanism in contemporary behavioral psychology.

LINGUISTIC ANALYSIS AND PERSONALITY THEORY

The *double-aspect* theory of Fechner, the nineteenth-century psychophysicist (Boring, 1950), and the *two-language* approach of *linguistic analysis* (Barbour, 1966) seemingly constitute solutions that are not dualistic, parallelistic, or monistic. These positions see mind and brain (body) as two aspects of the same process. Convenient though it may seem to reduce the problem to semantics, in reality mind and brain are either identical *or* nonidentical. Any position proposing them to be identical is reducible to monism, and any view proposing them to be nonidentical is reducible to dualism or to parallelism (Bittle, 1948).

PROCESS THEORIES OF PERSONALITY

More recent concepts that come close to that of formal causality are the *transcendent function* of Carl Jung, the *proprium* of Gordon Allport, and the *organicism* of Ian Barbour (Hall and Lindzey, 1957; Barbour, 1966). However, in the final analysis, these theorists reject formal causality and define their concepts in terms of process or function, thereby recapitulating Descartes. These positions, as well as all process theories of personality, are ultimately reducible to idealistic monism or to materialistic monism.

CRITIQUE

Idealism, the position that the materiality experienced is but a projection of the mind and that the mind alone possesses true existence, is a contradiction of empirical experience. If one were to stand on the tracks before an approaching locomotive, it would be difficult to be convinced that the consequent encounter was a projection of one's mind. It is equally difficult to accept evil behavior on the part of others as a projection of the observer's mind. The same is true of personal pain and suffering, as well as of suffering perceived in other individuals. Idealism, therefore, violates empirical experience.

An analysis of materialism, the position that man is pure matter and that therefore mind is a materialistic function of the brain, is found in later discussions of mechanism and vitalism and of the contrast between mind and brain. Suffice it to say here that materialism in contemporary psychology is a direct consequent of assuming the experimental method to be the only valid approach in studying man, an assumption already seen to be gratuitous and unnecessary.

As for Descartes's rejection of formal causality, what are the implications? The denial of substance underlying activity leaves synthesis without a synthesizer, integration without an integrator, organization without an organizer, extension without a subject to be extended, measurements without something to be measured, forces without a forcer, movement without a mover, change without something to change, activity without something to act, and thinking without a mind to think. To the contrary, however, reason demands something to underlie motion, to undergo change, to carry out activity—in other words, something in which transitory activities inhere. Furthermore, since activity, change, and motion are realities, the *substance* in which these processes inhere must also be a reality. The ontological principles of form and matter satisfy this demand of reason.

Descartes is also responsible for the contemporary psychologist's condemnation of dualism. The charges that dualists have introduced a "manikin," a "homunculus," a "man within the breast" (F. H. Allport, 1955; Hall and Lindzey, 1957), or a "deus ex machina" (Chaplin and Krawiec, 1960) should be directed only against *unnatural dualism*. These criticisms are inappropriate to *natural dualism*, which does not separate the organism into two independently existing parts. Formal causality, the basis of natural dualism, is unknown and unrecognized in contemporary psychology, and this ignorance is a heritage from Cartesian and seventeenth-century philosophy.

The dissatisfaction with the Cartesian premise is, in the author's opinion, one reason why the concept of the hypothetical construct has become popular with those who on theoretical grounds deny the existence of substance. The unreasonableness of bodily activity floating in space without a substantial source or substrate has compelled behavioral psychologists to speak once again of such entities as memory and mind, even though their actual existence is denied.

In regard to the physicist's contemporary equation of matter with energy, formal causality is still applicable. Where, for example, lies the distinction between the electron and the proton? Both embody energy. The difference lies in the *form* of energy, such that one is described in action as positive and the other negative.

In summary, then, formal causality adequately represents the basic nature of things, whether they be elemental particles of matter or human beings. Natural dualism, a consequence of formal causality, is the personality theory preferred by the Christian psychologist. The compatibility of this theory with all experimental evidence of contemporary behavioral psychology will be demonstrated in the chapters to follow. Furthermore, since this theory is internally consistent and compatible with observed behavioral data, it should be as acceptable as any other theory of personality (Hall and Lindzey, 1957). However, because of historical ignorance, as well as the bias of the behavioral psychologist in accepting the experimental approach as the only one valid, this theory of personality has been unjustly ignored in contemporary psychology.

THE PROBLEM OF SELF-IDENTITY

In view of the temporal changes that take place both physically and psychologically in the human organism, how is self-identity preserved? The body is completely renewed within ten years, and one need only reminisce in order to realize the changes that occur in one's attitudes, values, and learning processes through time.

William James, who took as a starting point the Cartesian position that rejected formal causality, attempted to save the idea of unity of behavior through time by defining consciousness as a stream of ideas, each idea passing on its identity to the next (James, 1890). However, this interpretation fails to explain what governs consciousness and directs the process. Again, physically speaking, what preserves the structural organization of the millions of bodily cells, such that a man is physically recognizable as the same person despite the passage of years and the replacement of bodily cells?

The denial of an underlying personality substrate will invariably result in the problem of explaining unity. Behavioral psychology, in Cartesian footsteps, has created a problem that does not actually exist. According to the theory of formal causality, the human person may be viewed from two aspects. One aspect is the unchanging nature of personality, and the other is that which does change. The renewal of actual bodily cells and the revision of ideas, attitudes, values, and experiences can be referred to as the *empirical personality*. The empirical personality includes all the changes, physical and psychological, produced environmentally through time. The other aspect of the human person is that which does not change, but which rather underlies change (Table 9). This is the substantial nature of man, composed of matter and form, which can be referred to as the *metaphysical personality*. The metaphysical personality is man's basic nature, which it-

Table 9.   **Theories of Self-Identity**

Theory	Definition of Self
Behavioral theory	Self is (*a*) the accumulative total or constellation of acquired changes, physical and psychological (empirical definition), or (*b*) the totality of human functions and processes.
Christian theory	Self includes not only the above aspects, but also a *metaphysical* aspect, namely, the unchanging substrate which underlies temporal change.

self does not change, but rather underlies change. It is the metaphysical personality that accounts for self-identity despite change and the passage of time. It is the metaphysical personality that also accounts for the stability and unchanging nature of the person, whether psychological, as in the case of basic intelligence, or physiological, as in the structural arrangement of bodily cells. Finally, the metaphysical personality accounts for the psychic trace and neurological trace involved in the memory process (T.V. Moore, 1939).

It is by virtue of the metaphysical personality, therefore, that one retains mental and physical self-identity, i.e., conscious realization that "I" am *substantially* the same person as "I" was ten years ago. The physical recognition by others of this fact has the same source. In summary, the personality *substantially* remains the same, though undergoing *empirical* change.

It should also be noted that most of the "self" theories proposed by contemporary psychologists are in this context either (*a*) empirical definitions of personality, if self is defined as the sum total or constellation of acquired *experiences*, or (*b*) the totality of the *functions* flowing from the metaphysical personality, although the source of these functions is denied any status of reality. Hall and Lindzey (1957) therefore rightly state that most contemporary personality theorists define the self or ego as a name for a *group of processes*. Indeed, Hall and Lindzey are bold enough to assert that the self is not a metaphysical or religious concept at all, but rather one that falls within the domain of scientific psychology. They are correct, of course, in that psychology should certainly study the self, but are incorrect in arbitrarily defining it as process alone, and they are imprudent in denying that self is an appropriate subject for study in philosophy and theology.

MAN AS MACHINE

Although the concept of man as machine found a place in early Greek philosophy, this viewpoint, termed *mechanism*, has received new impetus over the last twenty years. Cybernetics (Wiener, 1948; Ashby, 1966) and the application of computer electronics to physiological measurements led psychologists to consider the human brain itself to be a type of computer. It was quite easy to jump from the level of analogy to the level of identification. The brain was first described as analogous to a computer; it is now defined as such. The nervous system was once said to have electrical properties; it is now presented as consisting of electrical energy.

Is man merely a higher-order, highly complicated machine? If so, he is reducible to matter and subject to the laws of matter. This viewpoint is a modern interpretation of materialism, discussed previously. What is the alternative view? The interpretation opposed to mechanism is that of *vitalism*, the position that man is not matter alone, but is also composed of non-materiality (Donceel, 1965a). Vitalism contends that man is dualistic, but in a natural way. Vitalism is not to be confused with animism, the primitive appraisal of man's spirit as a little man within a man. In primitive animistic practice, for example, when a man died a hole would be made in his skull to permit the escape of his soul. Vitalism has been abused by mechanistic psychologists in the equation with primitive animism. Vitalism does not propose a magical life-stuff within the human person (K. Smith, 1958). On the contrary, the source of life, the vital principle, is to be identified in man with the formal cause, already discussed in relation to the theory of natural dualism. It should also be noted that the vital principle should not be identified with the efficient cause, a mistake on the part of some theorists that incorrectly leads to unnatural dualism (Donceel, 1965b).

BIOLOGICAL LIFE THEORIES

An outline of biological life theory is presented in Table 10. The two broad theories of *merism* (emphasis on cellular components) and *holism*

Table 10. **Biological Life Theory in Psychology**

| Merism | | Holism | |
Mechanistic	Vitalistic	Mechanistic	Vitalistic
Stimulus-response theorists	(Extinct)	Neo-Gestaltists	Plato
Behavioral psychologists		Field theorists	Aristotle
Cybernetics theorists		Psychoanalysts	Old Gestaltists
		Physiological psychologists	Wurzburg school
		Behavioral psychologists	Christian psychologists
		Humanistic psychologists	Humanistic psychologists
		Existential psychologists	Existential psychologists

(emphasis on the organic whole) can be further classified into mechanistic and vitalistic interpretations. The positions having the greatest popularity in contemporary psychological theory are mechanistic merism and mechanistic holism, both being examples of materialistic monism. The former position is held by many learning theorists, while the latter has appeal for clinical and personality theorists. Vitalistic holism finds favor with Christian psychologists, as well as with humanistic psychologists (Bugental, 1967; Severin, 1965).

VITALISM AS LIFE THEORY

The experimental method of science cannot be used to prove vitalism. This is the precise reason for the popularity of mechanism. Scientists prefer to deal with the concrete and tangible, not with the abstract and intangible. The *behavior patterns* of living things can be seen, but the *source* of such activities cannot be seen. It must be inferred. The method of immediate inference, then, is the procedure for arriving at the validity of vitalism. First, however, there must be the examination of empirical evidence.

Table 11.   Characteristics of Life and Nonlife

Living Cell	Nonliving Crystal
1. *Nutrition, metabolism* synthesis of anabolism with catabolism	1. *Static equilibrium* tendency to act in one direction only
2. *Growth and repair* cell increases growth from within; repairs injured tissue	2. *Accretion* growth by addition from environment
3. *Reproduction* produces a new being from its own substance	3. *Nonreproduction* new crystals added by the environmental medium
4. *Irreversibility* at death cannot be reconstructed	4. *Reversibility* can be destroyed and reconstituted

The contrasting activities of a cell and a crystal are given in Table 11. Four characteristics manifested by the living cell mark living things as distinct from those lacking life: nutrition, growth, reproduction, and irreversibility of the destruction of life. It is the presence of these activity patterns that warrants the identification of an object as being alive (Brachet,

1961). The vital principle is, in effect, the *difference* between a living body and a corpse. Subtract this factor, and death is the consequence. It should be noted, materially speaking, that the corpse still possesses electrical energy, yet life—indicated by nutrition, growth, and cellular activity—is absent.

Vitalism fits in well with the theory of formal causality and natural dualism. Man is composed of matter (body) and form (vital principle), united in one complete substance. Each is irreducible to the other, and each is incomplete without the other; both are required to produce the unitary substance called man. Vitalism is also compatible with the Christian concept of the resurrection of the body—the concept that the incomplete material element will someday be reunited with the incomplete spiritual element, once more to constitute the whole man.

SOUL, MIND, AND WILL

Man is surely matter. The electrons in his ear lobe are no different, as electrons, than those of chalk. But man is also surely something other than matter. He is vitalized matter. And that which vitalizes man renders him capable of nutrition, growth, and reproduction, as well as of other life processes such as perception and thought.

The vital principle is referred to by several names, depending on the life process in question. For example, the *mind* is the vital principle in its cognitive activity, the *will* is the life principle in its decision-making capacity, the *memory* is the life principle in its remembering process, and the *soul* is the vital principle in prayer activity, or communication with God. Mind, soul, will, memory, and vital principle are therefore identical. Vitalism does not divide man into a bundle of parts.

THE ANIMAL-MAN CONTINUUM

It has been said that Darwin "homogenized" the differences between animal and man, and that it is incorrect to posit man as essentially different from any animals from which he may have evolved (Atkinson, 1964). The Christian psychologist, however, points to evidence that man's vital principle is capable of functions far superior to those of the vital principles of other animals. And through the theological method an immortality unique to man can be established. However, even on the philosophical plane intrinsic differences between man and other living creatures can be demonstrated. The relevance of evolution to the origin of man will be discussed later in this chapter.

LIFE BEFORE BIRTH

A corollary of vitalism is that life for a new human organism begins at the moment the egg is fertilized by the sperm. The vital principle of the resultant zygote guides the one cell in its multiple division to the final formation of a mature individual. Human birth is not, therefore, the beginning of life but rather a transition in environment. (This transition is not necessary for all species of life, e.g., the frog egg is fertilized outside of the female parent.) The newborn baby does not become human with this transition; it is human from the beginning of its life as the zygote. (Similarly, the fertilized frog egg has essentially a "frog life," even though it first exists in only one cell.) It is erroneous to believe that a person "acquires" human nature. "Metaphysically" speaking, the organism is just as human when it is one cell as when it is composed of millions of cells, since the vital principle, as such, is present from the beginning. "Empirically" speaking, the physical components of the organism—brain, eyes, and so on—must be developed through time, and when the organism is able to live in an environment apart from the mother, birth occurs.

The human organism, therefore, is intrinsically human from the first moment of formation of the zygote. Destruction of this zygote is therefore actually the destruction of a human person, a person not recognizable extrinsically, but in essence entirely human. It is ridiculous, therefore, to say that abortion of the unborn child is not a destruction of human life, just as it would be ridiculous to say that the destruction of a frog egg or tadpole is not a destruction of a "frog life." The fact that a fetus is nonviable, i.e., cannot live apart from the mother's environmental nourishment, is no evidence to conclude it is nonhuman. The Christian psychologist, therefore, does not make the identification of human nature contingent on what is sensorially observable, but rather defines human nature in terms of what is intrinsically present.

The criterion of the presence of a recognizable human nature, e.g., the formation of a brain, or eyes, or limbs, as necessary for a being to be considered a human person, can be proved absurd from another point of view.

Consider for a moment the person born with missing limbs, or again, the amputee. Are they to be considered less than human? Should the individual who suffers cortical cellular impairment be considered so? Obviously not. Even the severely mentally retarded are intrinsically (metaphysically) human, although they do not behave or function normally because of improper or inadequate cerebral development (a defect in the empirical personality). That society tends, however, to evaluate human personality on the empirical (behavioral) level rather than on the metaphysical level is reflected in the sad neglect in treatment accorded the mental retardate or the institutionalized psychotic, both of whom are regarded as lacking the intrinsic dignity of a human being (Blatt and Kaplan, 1967). Society in this instance has fallen victim to a non-Christian interpretation of human nature.

EVOLUTION

Evolution is the process through which the present world came about (Figure 2). Dvelopment of our universe can be referred to as *cosmogenesis*, the evolution of our planet as *geogenesis*, the emergence of life as *biogenesis*, and the appearance of man as *anthropogenesis* (Francoeur, 1965; Teilhard de Chardin, 1959). The author will use the term *psycho-sociogenesis* to refer to the subsequent development of man and society to the present day, and hence into the future.

The evidence for evolution is quite compelling. Similarity of bodily structures on different phylogenetic levels of life, similarities in embryological development, vestigial remains in certain organisms, and similiarities in biochemical makeup seem to point to evolution as the process through which the present world developed (Francoeur, 1965; R. Moore, 1964).

EVOLUTION AND CREATION

Evolution as such is neither theistic nor atheistic, for it is process alone. To evolve means to change. Whether or not there is Intelligence directing the process of evolution is a philosophical problem, not a scientific one (J. E. Royce, 1961). Therefore, when scientists begin to expound on evolution as the consequence of "chance" factors, they are no longer speaking as scientists, but as philosophers. Since evolution of the past has never been

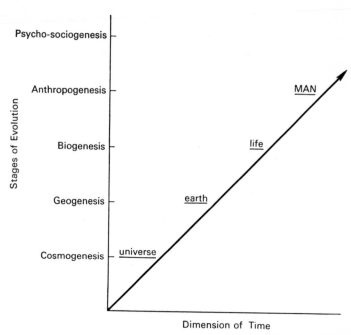

FIG. 2.   Evolutionary stages through time.

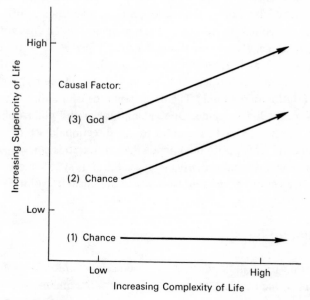

FIG. 3.   Causal theories of evolution.

empirically observed, it can never be "scientifically" demonstrated whether or not it was due to chance or to Intelligence. However, this problem *can* be philosophically examined, in an analysis of the *direction* evolution has taken. Three causel theories are prevalent today.

First is the position that evolution has followed a chance direction. It holds that the complexity of the phylogenetic scale should not be interpreted as going from "low" to "high," for each phylum is perfectly adapted to *its* particular environment. Hence, man should not be considered superior to the fish or the bird, for he has neither gills nor wings. Each organism, therefore, should be considered in reference to its unique adaptation to a special environment, and in this sense no organism is superior in essence to another. Thus, evolution and development of life follow a horizontal direction rather than an upward direction (Figure 3).

A second position is the recognition that evolution does follow an upward direction, that through time the phylogenetic scale does represent increasing superiority as well as complexity of life. However, this direction is also the result of pure chance and does not involve purpose or design. Both of these positions can be classified under materialistic evolutionary theory, or atheistic evolutionary theory.

A third position is the recognition that through time the phylogenetic scale not only reflects increasing superiority and complexity of the development of life, but also manifests direction, order, and purpose. Furthermore, the theory of evolution may explain what happened, but it does not explain *why*. For example, why should things survive? Whence comes the compulsion of a living thing to extend its life—and further, to perpetuate the life of the species? And still further, why should things evolve at all? And lastly, why is evolution directional? The orderly parade of life through the ages demands an intelligent guide. One paleontologist and philosopher, Teilhard de Chardin (1959), has referred to this directional path of evolution as *orthogenesis*. This position contends that evolution is guided by Intelligence, or God, and that the process of evolution is synonymous with the process of creation. Some philosophers even consider evolution to be a proof of God's existence (Schoonenberg, 1964).

LIFE FROM NONLIFE

According to evolutionary theory, the carbon molecule evolved into amino acids, the building blocks of life. From the amino acids emerged proteins and then the first life forms, the one-celled protozoa. These in turn evolved into metazoa, and thus began the sequence of plants, animals, and ultimately man.

Whether or not this process was due to chance or to Intelligence is again a problem beyond the domain of science, and revelant to the three philosophical causal theories of evolution. According to the first and second theories, life spontaneously emerged from some chance combination of material elements under certain favorable conditions in the distant past (Wald, 1954). It follows that living things are more complex than nonliving things but not essentially different. Even man is thereby reducible to matter. The third theory proposes that chance alone could not produce life, but that God *could* direct the emergence of life from matter. This position permits the possibility that living matter is essentially different from, and superior to, nonliving matter. The analysis of the properties of life and nonlife, in the previous discussion of vitalism and mechanism, verifies this possibility.

THE LIFE-NONLIFE CONTINUUM

Some substances—for instance, a tobacco virus—are capable of both reproduction and crystallization. Are they therefore alive or not? Such objects constitute difficulties in identification, perhaps to be clarified as instruments of biological observation, such as the electronic microscope, are made more precise. However, the vitalist contends that any object, no matter how small, is either alive or not alive, and cannot be both simultaneously, since the two states of existence are mutually exclusive. If an object has the capacities for metabolism, growth, and reproduction, it is a living thing, whether or not such behavior can be observed. It should be noted that the *capacity* for such activities is the only requisite for life. These capacities need not be active in order for a substance to be considered a living substance. An example is seeds that have been dormant for a lengthy period and not manifesting active behavior (J. E. Royce, 1961).

Materialistic evolutionary theory has led to the hypothesis of a continuum between life and nonlife, i.e., living things differ from nonliving things merely in complexity rather than in essence. In the middle of the continuum lie substances that are supposedly both alive and not alive. As noted, this line of thought involves a contradiction. The exclusion of a

Creator by materialistic evolutionary theory leaves this theory with the compulsion to assert that "somehow or other" matter accounts exclusively for the origin of life, and therefore life (effect) cannot be essentially different from matter (its cause). Theistic evolutionary theory does not suffer from this compulsion, since this position asserts that God is the efficient cause of the emergence of life from matter.

Another criticism of materialistic evolutionary theory involves the interpretation of the nature of a continuum. There is a basic fallacy in assuming that a continuum actually exists. A continuum is a mathematical abstraction, just as are mathematical points and lines. Continuums do not exist in reality; they are descriptive mental concepts imposed on reality. For example, intelligence scores are discrete, tangible entities, even though they form a plotted distribution that can be mathematically described as a normal distribution, a continuity. Therefore, to posit a continuity scale with nonlife at one end, life at the other, and a middle point for items both living and nonliving is pure conjecture, unfounded in fact.

MULTILEVEL ANALYSIS AND PROCESS PHILOSOPHY

The assumption of the continuum between life and nonlife is used by process theorists in multilevel analysis. Thus mechanism is viewed as a one-level metaphysics and vitalism as a two-level metaphysics. Barbour (1966) proposes *organicism* as a third alternative. Organicism assumes a continuity between life and nonlife, as well as between forms of life on different levels of complexity. There are no sharp boundaries, no separate strata in nature.

The concept of the continuum as a reality existing apart from the mind has already been questioned. If organicism does not recognize essential differences (differences in essence, substance) between living things and nonliving things, then this position is reduced to a sophisticated form of mechanism.

The concept of multilevel analysis can be adopted, however, in reflecting essential differences between life and nonlife, as well as different levels of complexity of life. Such a use of this approach, however, places it in a perspective different from that intended by the originators.

LABORATORY PRODUCTION OF LIFE

Will man someday "create" life from nonliving matter? Biochemists have succeeded in producing deoxyribonucleic acid (DNA) (Allfrey and Mirsky, 1961), as well as what appears to be a living virus (Goulian, Kornberg, and Sinsheimer, 1967). Does this support materialistic or atheistic theory regarding the origin of life? It means that man may someday be able to *replicate* that evolutionary process that occurred so many eons ago (Donceel, 1965a; Teilhard de Chardin, 1959). It does not mean that man can *create* life, since the structural components are already existent. He only manipulates the factors involved in the production of life. His success could also be indirect evidence that intelligence is required to produce life from existing elements, thus tending to support the theistic explanation of the original event long ago: God originally produced life, and did so from matter that he initially created.

THE EVOLUTION OF MAN

The emergence of man from an animal ancestor is seen differently in the three philosophical interpretations of evolution previously discussed. From the two materialistic points of view, man differs from his animal ancestor merely in complexity and is not essentially different. From the theistic point of view, the human life principle is essentially different from that of any prehuman predecessor. At this point theistic theory falls into two camps. The traditional school contends that God created the first human soul and infused it into a prehuman animal body *after* that body had evolved to a degree of development preordained by the Creator. The human soul, therefore, did not itself evolve, although the human body may have. A contemporary theistic interpretation is that of Teilhard de Chardin (1959), who maintains that God's creation of the human soul occurred in the evolutionary process itself. Spirit evolved from matter, and the human soul did likewise. These two theistic views are in fundamental agreement on the point that the human soul is intrinsically and essentially superior to all other previously evolved lifeforms. The views differ in the temporal aspect of creation. The traditional school contends that God created the human soul at the point of time in evolution when man was ordained to appear on the face of the earth, whereas the contemporary school maintains that God from the beginning of evolution instilled in matter the capability of eventually evolving a human soul. Teilhard de Chardin accordingly proposes that as evolution progressed, there occurred a shift from physical energy to psychic energy, from materiality to spirituality (Teilhard de Chardin, 1959; Francoeur, 1965). The contemporary interpretation has criticized the traditional interpretation for making God appear to be a rather awkward designer, in that he apparently had to "intervene" in the evolutionary process to create the human soul (Francoeur, 1965; Donceel, 1965a). However, the traditionalists reply that God can create at any point of time he pleases, and that if he did so, it would not be intervention at all, but rather the plan he chose to follow.

THE FUTURE EVOLUTION OF MAN

Now that man has appeared on earth, where does evolution go from here? Will life forms higher than the human evolve? Further biological development is unlikely, from a Christian point of view, since it is reasonable to infer that God would not have become incarnate when he did (in the person of Christ) if human evolution had not yet reached its biological zenith. However, it would seem that evolution could continue on a level different from that of biological change. This nonbiological evolution can be termed *psycho-sociogenesis*. (See Figure 2.) As with past evolution, Teilhard and others have proposed this shift in the emphasis of continuing evolution from the physical and biological plane to the psychological and psychic plane (Francoeur, 1965).

Where will human evolution culminate? From a Christian viewpoint, God is the Alpha and the Omega, and therefore he is both the ultimate efficient cause and the ultimate final cause. Human evolution, accordingly, is directed toward God as the ultimate goal (Teilhard de Chardin, 1959, 1965; Francoeur, 1965; Donceel, 1965a; Schoonenberg, 1964). This assertion does not mean man will become God, the error of pantheism, but rather that man is to evolve to the point where he will be prepared for life in the Divine Presence, theologically referred to as the Beatific Vision. From another aspect, man is to evolve to the point where he will be most like Christ, the God-Man. In a future chapter, this becoming-like-Christ will be seen to be the vocation of the Christian.

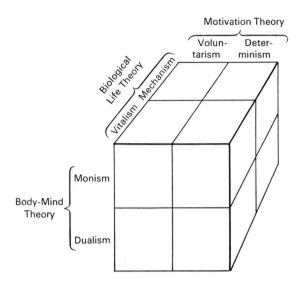

FIG. 4. Theories of human nature.

CIRCLE, ARROW, AND SPIRAL

Francoeur (1965) presents an interesting contrast of trends in past philosophical thought with contemporary evolutionary thought. He characterizes Greek philosophy as being fixed, closed, and symbolized by a circle. The Biblical revelation of the Judeo-Christian world vision is directional and linear, symbolized by an arrow. Then there are combinations of the two, the best of which is Teilhard's synthesis. Teilhard's integration of scientific evolutionary theory with Christian philosophical theory can be symbolized by a spiral. This combination of the best in a cyclic world vision with the best in a linear world vision can be further described as an ascending and converging spiral (Francoeur, 1965).

Whether or not Teilhard de Chardin has produced a philosophy of man drastically different from that of Aristotle and Aquinas (the basis of the personality theory of natural dualism presented in the present chapter) can be disputed. Donceel (1965b), cited by Francoeur (1965), maintains that Teilhard's "radial level" of causality is comparable to Aquinas' final causality. Thus, even though Aquinas did not write of evolution as such, it is still compatible with his doctrine of final causality, which is that all beings are directed toward goals. Evolution adds the dimension of time to the concept of final causality. To do justice to Francoeur's analysis, however, the reader is urged to read his view of Teilhard's contribution to a philosophy of human nature.

A SUMMING UP

Theories of the nature of man can be summarized in a threefold classification, embracing *body-mind theory*, *biological life theory*, and *motivation theory* (Figure 4). Motivation theory will be discussed in a Chapter 7.

Chapter 6

Mind and Brain

A corollary of the vitalistic position was that the life principle, from the moment of conception, operates within the single fertilized cell, the zygote, to develop it into the final product, the mature organism. In man, therefore, the human life principle is present at the moment of conception, guiding the development of the zygote through embryonic and fetal stages to the environmental transition point known as birth. The vital principle, existing prior to neurological development in the embryo, is therefore responsible for the development of the brain. It also follows that thinking, a vital process, is a function of the vital principle, as are all life activities. The brain, in consequence, is the instrument through which the vital principle operates, as is true of other bodily parts. From the vitalistic point of view, the brain is not the source of thought processes, a supposition maintained by mechanists. For example, Gordon Murray contends that not only thinking but also personality is a function of the brain (Hall and Lindzey, 1957), and Wolman proposes that mental processes evolve from higher somatic structures (Wolman, 1960).

It can further be shown that ideation, the formation of abstract ideas and concepts, is exclusively a function of the vital principle, and that the brain merely serves in preparatory prerequisite activity, i.e., in the formation of *percepts* from which the *concept* is abstracted by the vital principle.

THE PRINCIPLE OF CAUSALITY

Only one gallon of liquid can be contained in a one-gallon pail. A nickel will purchase only a nickel's worth of candy. These simple examples illustrate the relation between cause and effect. This relation, expressed as the Principle of Causality, is that an effect cannot be greater than its cause, or, in other words, effects are proportional to their causes. A one-gallon pail cannot hold two gallons of liquid, nor can a nickel buy a dime's worth of candy.

The Principle of Causality is relevant to the demonstration of the incapability of the brain to produce an idea. That is, it can be shown that an idea (effect) is of a higher order than the brain (presumed cause), and that therefore the former cannot be accounted for by the latter. Consequently, there is the need for a proper cause (the vital principle). Insistence that the brain produces ideas or concepts will be shown to be a violation of the Principle of Causality; the effect cannot be greater than its cause.

CONCEPT FORMATION

Concept formation, or ideation, is the highest capability of a human being. This activity sets man apart from all other animals and is characteristic exclusively of him. It is a common error of many psychology texts to fail to differentiate thinking as a human process from thinking on the animal level. This distinction will be discussed at the end of this chapter. The immediate point to be illustrated is the formation of a concept or idea in the thinking process.

Consider the ordinary playground item called the seesaw or teeter-totter. If two children of equal weight were to be placed opposite each other at equal distances from the center of the seesaw, they would balance each other. This simple example illustrates what is known in physics as the principle of the fulcrum. The equation expressing the principle is *mass* × *distance* = *mass* × *distance* (Figure 5).

An indefinite number of situations could illustrate this principle. For example, a mass of ten pounds placed five feet from the point of balance would equal a mass of five pounds placed ten feet away on the other side ($10 \times 5 = 5 \times 10$). The balance underlying the principle of the fulcrum can be summed up in one word: equality. One side equals the other side. An *understanding* of the principle of the fulcrum is then, in essence,

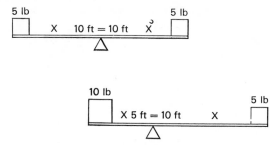

FIG. 5.   Examples of a fulcrum.

an understanding of the relation of equality. A *concept* has been formed.

It should further be noted that the understanding of the concept of equality, even though arrived at by an analysis of discrete empirical examples, can now be retained and understood *as such*, apart from the situations from which it has been derived. In other words, the understanding of equality is an *experience in itself*. To illustrate, the tangible material used prior to the formation of this concept can be eliminated, ultimately leaving the concept as a separate and final experience (Figure 6). Successive steps in the illustration are removal of (*a*) a specific example, (*b*) the balance line, (*c*) the point of balance, and lastly (*d*) the symbol of equality. The question could then be asked: Does one still understand, as an experience in itself, the meaning of equality? The answer is in the affirmative.

It is this experience of the meaning of the relationship called equality which is offered as illustrative of a concept, or idea. The reader familiar

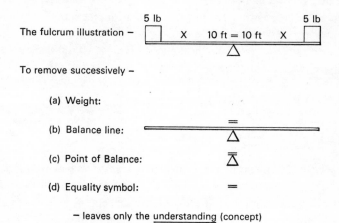

FIG. 6.   Illustration of a concept.

with the history of psychology may recognize here the similarity between this analysis of conceptual meaning and the "imageless thought" model of the Würzburg school (Chaplin and Krawiec, 1960; Wolman, 1960; F. H. Allport, 1955; T. V. Moore, 1939).

BRAIN AND CONCEPT

In order to evaluate the mechanistic supposition that the brain produces a concept, it is necessary to examine the basic properties of the factors involved. The essential characteristics of brain and concept are presented in Table 12. Whereas the brain is basically dimensional, quantitative, and material, the concept is free of these limitations. It is this very freedom that assigns the concept to a higher order of existence than the brain.

Table 12.   Properties of Brain and Concept

Brain	Concept
Dimensional (volume, size, shape)	Nondimensional
Quantitative (weight, density, color, number of cells)	Nonquantitative
Material (matter, molecular structure)	Nonmaterial, Immaterial

This superiority in the order of existence is essential to the distinction between brain and concept. Since the concept is of a higher order of existence it cannot be an effect produced by the brain, a variable on a lower level of existence. Such a claim violates the Principle of Causality, for the effect can never be greater than its cause. In conclusion, then, the brain cannot be the cause of the concept.

What, therefore, produces the concept? It is the vital principle, in a final exclusive act, terminating a sequence of activity initially involving the brain.

THE NATURE OF MIND

The vital principle in its thinking activity can be referred to as the mind. The mind, as the source of intellection, must be able to account for the observed characteristics of its product, the concept. That is, the mind itself must be nondimensional, nonquantitative, and nonmaterial. That is precisely why it cannot be detected by a quantitative method, such as the microscopic examination of brain cells. The existence of the mind can be proved only by the method of immediate inference, after a logical analysis of empirically observed facts.

Where is the mind located? The location of something is unfortunately associated with the placement of material things. The mind, however, by nature cannot be quantitatively localized; it can only be spatially localized. It is a meaningless question to ask for the quantitative, dimensional locus of a nonquantitative, nondimensional reality. The mind (vital principle) cannot be quantitatively localized; it can only be spatially localized. It is within the human person.

An interesting parallel problem is the location of consciousness. As T. V. Moore (1939) has pointed out, consciousness is retained after the thalamus, hypothalamus, right cerebral hemisphere, left cerebral hemisphere, or even both frontal lobes are removed. Therefore, consciousness also is obviously not entirely a function of brain, nor can it be quantitatively or exclusively located in the brain.

THE REJECTION OF THE MIND

Why, then, do many psychologists reject the existence of the mind? There are several reasons (Table 13).

(1). Contemporary non-Christian psychologists have adopted E. L. Thorndike's axiom that whatever exists exists in quantity and therefore can be measured. Accordingly, any postulated nonquantitative reality does not

Table 13. Objections to Reality of Mind

(1) Assumption of existence in terms of quantity alone
(2) Assumption of mechanistic life theory
(3) Inability to understand nature of contact of immaterial reality with material reality
(4) Appeal to future knowledge of brain function
(5) Identification of percept with concept

exist. The Christian psychologist considers this axiom a philosophical statement, not a scientific one. For a theorist to say he is interested only in quantitative factors would be scientifically permissible, but to deny the existence of all things nonquantitative is unscientific, unnecessary, and a purely arbitrary position.

(2). Mechanism, again by assumption, precludes the possibility of the existence of mind. The Christian answer to mechanism is the evidence for vitalism.

(3). The inability to understand the working relationship between mind, an immaterial reality, and brain, a material reality, is another reason given for rejection of mind. However, it is unreasonable to reject a reasonable fact merely because it cannot be fully understood. Electricity, magnetism, gravity, and many other phenomena are accepted as reality, yet no man has yet fully understood the nature of these existing realities. The proof of the *existence* of a fact and the *understanding* of the nature of that fact should not be confused. At present, the relationship of mind to brain can only be described, as noted in the discussion of formal causality. Perhaps this relationship will someday be clearly understood—but perhaps not. Furthermore, it is a scientific sin of intellectual pride to presume that man can know everything, or that someday he will know everything. There is no evidence to support the compulsive acceptance of such an omnipotent presumption.

(4). But, it is sometimes argued, thought *must* be a function of brain, although at present the process is unknown. This compulsion is also unscientific; indeed, it could be described as superstitious behavior. It is really a desperate statement on the part of those who by assumption have ruled out the possibility of nonmaterial reality. The "someday we'll know" attitude is reasonable only when evidence to solve a problem is unavailable. But when this position is taken because arbitrary assumptions make available evidence inadmissible, it becomes an irrational point of view.

(5). A final rejection of mind rests in the failure to differentiate the sensory percept from the intellectual concept, a distinction to be discussed next.

CONCEPTS AND PERCEPTS

One reason why contemporary psychologists consider man as only a higher-order animal, different in degree rather than essentially different from other animals, is the failure to distinguish the nature of human thinking from that of animal thinking. The confusion between the percept and the concept, originating in the seventeenth-century empiricism of Locke and Hume (Moore, 1939), is reflected today in the behavioristic model for experiments in concept formation (Chaplin and Krawiec, 1960). The generic application of the term *thinking* to both human and animal cognition may have fortified this error (Ruch, 1967; Geldard, 1962). However, there is no evidence to indicate that animals can form concepts or ideas (Morgan, 1961). Animal learning can be explained on the perceptual level and does not require functioning on the conceptual level. What, then, is the difference between perceptual thinking and conceptual thinking?

The *percept* is the synthesis of the various sensations received through the different sense modalities. Consider, for example, an old-fashioned steam locomotive getting under way. In addition to the visual image, there are the auditory sensation of noise, the olfactory stimulation by smoke fumes, the sensation of heat, the kinesthetic experience of vibration, and possibly the gustatory detection of smoke. Now the operations of individual sense modalities are not experienced in isolation. Rather, these various kinds of sensations are experienced as a whole, such that one might remark, "That locomotive is about to start." The unity of this experience is consequent to the synthesis of sensations involved, and it is this sensory synthesis that should be termed a percept (Moore, 1939). Percepts may also involve *sensorially perceived relations*. The rat jumping to one of two differently sized triangles may be taught to choose the larger of the two to escape shock. In a consequent choice situation in which the formerly larger triangle is now the smaller of a pair, the animal will again choose the larger, ignoring in this instance what was formerly the correct specific response (Figure 7). No formation of a concept is necessary to explain this type of learning. The relationship between the two triangles can be observed on the sensory or perceptual level.

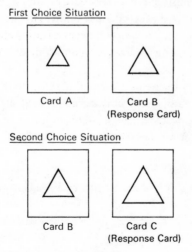

FIG. 7.   Relative size-discrimination learning.

The failure to distinguish thinking on the perceptual level from thinking on the conceptual level has resulted in psychology's lumping man and animal together, as far as their cognitive natures are concerned, and has led to the rejection of essential differences. To maintain that animals form ideas or concepts is a violation of the canon of parsimony, i.e., the simplest explanation of a phenomenon should be preferred over more complicated and unnecessary interpretations. Animal thinking and animal learning can be adequately explained in terms of perceptual activity. To ascribe ideational behavior to animals other than man is unwarranted. This capacity has been demonstrated by man alone, and it accounts for his unique creativity, progress, and advance in civilization.

MIND AND BRAIN

In the discussion of the distinction between brain and concept, the fulcrum was used to illustrate the derivation of the concept. Now, the pictures drawn of the seesaw, and the words written about it induced visual sensations in the reader. These sensations were accumulatively synthesized into a percept, a sensory understanding. The brain was responsible for the formation of this percept. However, at this point the mind performed an operation uniquely its own, the *abstraction* of the understanding of equality. The experience of abstraction and its consequence, the concept, were seen to be nondimensional, nonquantitative, and nonmaterial. The mind (vital principle) and the brain (vitalized matter) worked together, therefore, in a natural cooperative sequence of events. Both were needed for concept formation, the brain as a preliminary condition, and the mind as the ultimate cause.

How mind and brain are coordinated in this activity is, perhaps, forever unknowable. The contact of immateriality with materiality has always been a challenging problem, the resolution of which may well lie beyond human capability and understanding.

LINGUISTIC ANALYSIS AND PROCESS PHILOSOPHY

From both a linguistic-analysis point of view and a process point of view, mind and brain are considered to be not distinct entities but rather two aspects of the same process of events (Barbour, 1966). These positions are similar to the double-aspect theory of Fechner (Boring, 1950) and were mentioned earlier in the discussion of personality theory. Suffice it to say that such views ignore the essential differences between mind and brain, and are reducible to monism.

MAN WITHOUT BRAIN

As a corollary, it should be noted that the partial absence of brain in a person does not detract from his intrinsic value as a human being. Although brain surgery can reduce a person to a vegetative level of *functioning*, that person has not lost his human *nature*. No more so has a paralyzed or sightless person. The vital principle is still present in all of these instances, even though the bodily condition necessary for the expression of certain vital functions is absent. This fact has importance for the ethical treatment of individuals in such cases as brain-injury. Too often the clinical psychologist and the physician make an evaluation of brain-deprived patients as less than human. The severely mentally retarded are often regarded similarly. Because these unfortunate individuals do not *behave* in a normal human manner does not mean they are not human. This is the fundamental error of behaviorism as an ethical evaluation of human nature. Such patients deserve the same respect for the dignity of human nature as that rendered normally functioning persons. Loss of this clinical perspective largely accounts for the animalistic evaluation of the institutionalized mentally ill. Changes in the empirical personality of the individual do not detract from the intrinsic value of his metaphysical personality. It is the latter by which the dignity of man should be measured.

Chapter 7

Motivation and Reinforcement

The story of the passing of the concept of instinct from psychology is well known (Bindra, 1959; Boring, 1950; Cofer and Appley, 1964). As early as 1924, Bernard enumerated several thousand "instincts," pointing out the disagreements and diversities of definition. Other investigators interpreted some of the so-called instincts as learned behavior patterns, e.g., the "instinct to wage war."

THE REJECTION OF INSTINCT

The rejection of instinct in psychology rested not only on confusion in definition, but also on criticism of apparently circular statements such as, Animals hoard because of the instinct to hoard. However, in defense of instinct, it may be said that the historical interest in this variable stemmed from the effort to answer the inquiry, Why? Why do animals hoard food? Not because it is instinctive, but rather in order to survive. Why do birds build nests? To provide the prerequisites for perpetuating the species. Why do salmon swim to fresh waters to spawn? Because the eggs would die in salt water. Why is the homeostatic condition sought? And so on and on. Thus, true instinct theorists were interested in the Why of *final causality*.

75

This form of causality is also referred to as teleology (from the Greek *telos*, or goal). Psychologists, however, became dissatisfied with answers referring to the future, and, in the shift from the influence of philosophy to that of science, they became interested rather in the neurological process involved. That is, there was change of interest from the Why (final causality) to the How (formal causality). Most contemporary psychologists studying instinct today are therefore physiologically oriented.

A second development in the instinct controversy was the introduction of the term *instinctive behavior*. This step made instinct even more tangible and susceptible to quantifiable observation, and can be attributed to the influence of behaviorism. A third stage, even more recent, was the replacement of *instinctive behavior* with the term *primary drive*. Learning theorists are responsible for this development. The introduction of a new term permitted a new definition free of the misunderstandings historically associated with the term *instinct*. The concept of primary drive was reserved for unlearned patterns of motivated behavior, while secondary drive was used to refer to motivated behavior that is learned. The two kinds of motivation can be respectively illustrated by the hunger drive and the drive for social prestige.

NATURE OF PRIMARY DRIVE

The various current interpretations of the nature of instinct or primary drive can be discussed in terms of S-R (stimulus-response) and S-O-R (stimulus-organism-response) theory (Figure 8). The S-R position is exemplified by Skinner's descriptive behaviorism, for which drive is that behavior or response consequent to deprivation of some stimulus (Skinner, 1953). The S-O-R neurological position is illustrated by Woodworth and Schlosberg (1954) and the ethologists Cofer and Appley (1964), for whom drive is basically physiological activity. The interpretation of *O* as being the underlying substance from which psychological and neurological activity stem is the position of the vitalistic psychologist. It is interesting to note that all positions other than the vitalistic one are ultimately reducible to S-R behavioristic theory. The relationship of such theory to the vitalism-mechanism controversy is further presented in Table 14.

In summary, instinct or primary drive is considered by behavioristically oriented psychologists to consist of behavior alone. The vitalistic psychologist, on the other hand, views instinct in greater depth. He sees it as

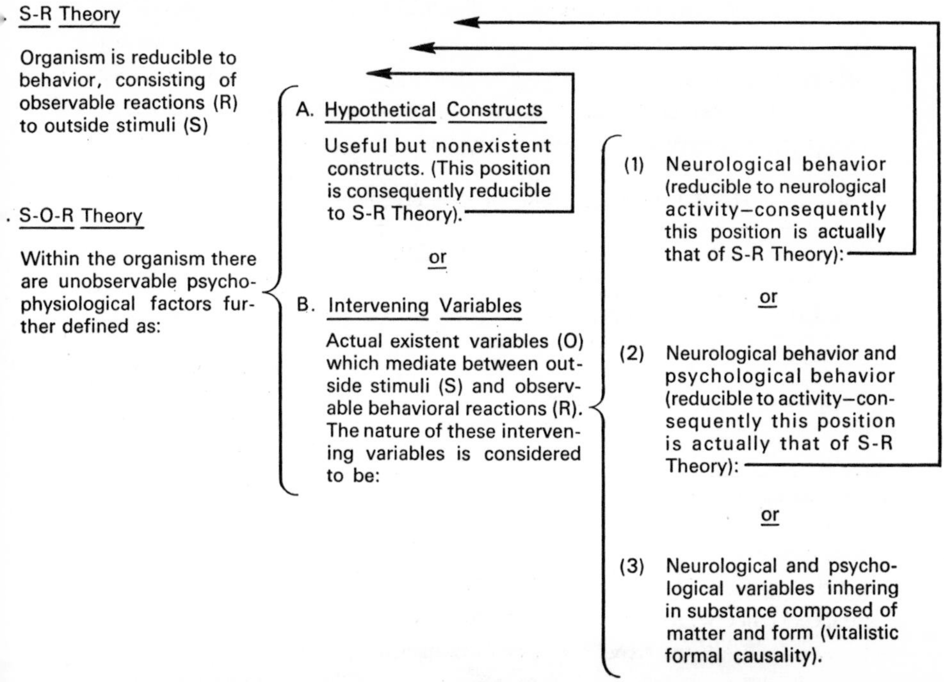

S-R Theory

Organism is reducible to behavior, consisting of observable reactions (R) to outside stimuli (S)

S-O-R Theory

Within the organism there are unobservable psycho-physiological factors fur-ther defined as:

A. Hypothetical Constructs

Useful but nonexistent constructs. (This position is consequently reducible to S-R Theory).

or

B. Intervening Variables

Actual existent variables (O) which mediate between out-side stimuli (S) and observ-able behavioral reactions (R). The nature of these interven-ing variables is considered to be:

(1) Neurological behavior (reducible to neurological activity—consequently this position is actually that of S-R Theory):

or

(2) Neurological behavior and psychological behavior (reducible to activity—con-sequently this position is actually that of S-R Theory):

or

(3) Neurological and psycho-logical variables inhering in substance composed of matter and form (vitalistic formal causality).

FIG. 8.   Psychological theory in terms of S-R and S-O-R classification.

Table 14.   S-R and S-O-R Theory as Related to Biological Life Theory

Psychological Theory	Life Theory Mechanism	Vitalism
S-R	behavior only	—
S-O-R	neurological *O*	neurological and psychological *O*

ultimately rooted in the substance of the organism, serving the purpose of survival of the individual and of the species. Survival in this sense is a form of causality (final causality).

THE NATURE OF REINFORCEMENT OR REWARD

Reinforcement theory can be classified under the same model used for drive theory. On the behavioral level, exemplified by Skinner (1953), rein-forcement is defined as that state of affairs occurring when a response tends to be repeated. Thus, the contiguity of stimulus and response, together with the subsequent repetition of the response, indicate that reinforcement has occurred (Bindra, 1959) (Table 15). The hypothetical construct theorist, e.g., Hull (1943), contends that reinforcement occurs whenever a drive is reduced. The drive and its reduction, however, are imaginary constructs.

Table 15.   The Behavioristic Model of Reinforcement*

Stimulus	Rate of Response	
Event	Increased R	Decreased R
S added	Food presented (positive reinforcement)	Shock presented (punishment, *or* negative reinforcement
S removed	Shock-escape (Negative reinforcement *or* positive reinforcement)	Food removed (negative reinforcement and extinction)

* Patterned after Bindra (1959)

This position is therefore reducible to that of behaviorism. The vitalistic psychologist would define reinforcement as the *experience* of satisfaction, an experience which, even though unobservable by others, is nevertheless known through introspection and is consequently existent and real. It is through inferential reasoning that vitalists consider animals also to experience some kind of satisfaction. Though the experience itself is unobservable, it can be inferred from behavior that is observed, e.g., a cat's purring.

WHAT REINFORCES?

Why are some things rewarding or reinforcing, and other things not? The descriptive behaviorism of Skinner's type cannot answer this question, since the study of S-R relationships will tell what reinforcers there are, but not why they function as such. Drive-reductionists would answer that stimuli become reinforcers when they reduce needs, e.g., food reduces hunger drive. Presumably, the process is neurological. Pleasure-pain theorists contend that the pleasantness of the experience, independent of drive-reduction, constitutes reinforcement (Bindra, 1939). Young's hedonic-quality hypothesis (Young, 1961) is an example of this position. It has been shown that rat learning occurs from saccharine reinforcement and morphine reinforcement, both substances being nonnutrient (nondrive-reducing) in nature. A third explanation is offered by consummatory-response theorists, who propose that it is the response rather than the food that reinforces (Bindra, 1939).

Experiments with throat fistula, in which food passes through the mouth of the animal but is removed prior to reaching the stomach, illustrate the extremes to which consummatory-response experimentalists have gone to prove that drive-reduction is unnecessary to the reinforcement process. This approach would have been unnecessary if behavioral experimentalists would accept (*a*) the simple facts of introspection (food tastes good, and therefore eating is rewarding) and (*b*) the legitimacy of inferring conscious experience in animals from external behavior that is observable. This last solution to the question of why reinforcers reinforce is the one maintained by vitalists, who contend that both drive-reduction and the variables of affective and sensory pleasure underlie the process of reinforcement. On the human level, this position can be verified by introspection. On the animal level, it must be inferred.

PURPOSE OR GOAL-DIRECTION IN BEHAVIOR

The question of intrinsic purpose in goal-directed behavior is ignored by the mechanistically inclined behaviorist, because this aspect is precluded from any system restricted to the behavioral level. The contrasting positions of vitalism and mechanism on this point are given in Table 16. Whereas mechanists accept only the objective or behavioral definition of purpose, vitalists include the subjective definition of the experience of purpose (Bindra, 1939). While purpose for the mechanists simply means behavior that is goal-directed, the vitalist emphasizes in addition the experience of intention, of a preconceived plan, and the awareness of purpose concerning the goal sought.

Table 16. Definitions of Purposive or Goal-Directed Behavior

Objective Definition	Objective + Subjective Definition
Mechanism: behavior directed toward a goal	Vitalism: behavior directed toward a goal for purpose of survival, and, in higher life forms, the experience of intention or awareness of purpose

To illustrate, consider the rat seeking food in a T-maze. If the variables of food-deprivation and activity toward the food box, or goal, are present, the behaviorist would describe the rat's response pattern as being goal-directed. The vitalist would add that after several trials and consequent learning of the correct response to the food box, the rat begins to experience purpose and intention when the correct response is made. This conclusion, of course is based on inference that the rat possesses awareness of its behavior. The mechanist, not willing to go beyond what can be externally observed, would not agree. When he speaks of purposive behavior, therefore, he does not mean the same thing as the vitalist does.

ANIMALS' AWARENESS OF PURPOSE

The vitalist contends that higher forms of animal life possess awareness because of the behavioral responses that *can* be observed and that justify this inference. For example, the overt response pattern of a rat motivated by electric shock markedly resembles the human behavior pattern in an identical situation. Palpitation, perspiration, and trembling indicate to the vitalist that the animal is experiencing fear, and that subsequently the animal experiences intention or purpose when it learns to escape the shock situation. Therefore, the vitalist denies that he is being anthropomorphic in attributing emotional awareness to the animal in such a situation. Obviously, however, this inference is not justifiable further down the phylogenetic scale—for example, in the case of insect behavior. Is there purpose, then, in such behavior? The vitalist would still answer in the affirmative, for even though the insect can be assumed to lack awareness, purpose is still served, in that survival is attained through the learned and unlearned (instinctive) behavior of insects.

THE FUTURE INFLUENCING THE PRESENT

How, the mechanist asks, can future goals influence present behavior? That is, how can something presently nonexistent have an effect on present motivation? Furthermore, there is no need, the mechanist continues, to resort to the future to explain the present, for past learning, conditioning, and stimulus generalization adequately account for animal behavior that is seemingly influenced by future goals.

The vitalist, in answer to these statements, agrees that past learning can explain goal-directed behavior in situations wherein opportunity for learning has already occurred, i.e., that the goal has been experientially learned. But there is still left unexplained the instance of goal-directed behavior in the absence of opportunity for learning, namely, instinctive behavior that seeks a goal prior to any association with that goal. Other examples of unlearned goal-directed behavior are those of natural growth, such as the development of wings on a bird. For the young nestling, flying is a future goal nonexistent at the time wings are being formed. Another example is the spider's development of spinnerets for future webs yet to be spun.

Therefore, concludes the vitalist, in animals there is purposive behavior referring to future goals as yet nonexistent. How is this? The solution lies in the vital principle, which *does* exist in the present. From the moment of conception the vital principle guides and develops the organism to its adult fulfillment. Purposive behavior is, therefore, an intrinsic function of the vital principle. The mechanist, in precluding the vital principle and defining animal (including man) as but a complex machine, is faced with a problem of his own making, the explanation of purposive behavior. This discussion illustrates once more the difficulties in which psychologists find themselves after adopting arbitrary, unnecessary premises.

FINAL AND FORMAL CAUSALITY

In conclusion, the failure of contemporary psychology to recognize the role of final causality (teleology, goal-seeking, purpose) in behavior has led to the redefinition of instinct or primary drive in terms of formal causality alone—that is, in terms of the physiological, neurological, and homeostatic processes involved. The attempt, however, to reduce the Why in behavior to the How in behavior is a methodological error. The Why in behavior is ultimately survival, which can be understood only in terms of final causality. It, too, is therefore a legitimate area of investigation in psychology and should not be arbitrarily excluded by the unnecessary assumptions of behaviorism.

THE FINAL GOAL IN HUMAN BEHAVIOR

With regard to final causality in human behavior, questions arise concerning man's ultimate goal. What thread should tie together and synthesize intermediate goals? What should be the coordinating factor to give meaning to human existence? These questions involve final causality, or teleology, in its ultimate form. One approach to the answer is the analysis of a universal human characteristic—the drive for security.

Although all men will agree that security is essential to human happiness and underlies all motivation, there is divided opinion on the definition of this need. The various interpretations can be grouped in a threefold classification, embracing the three kinds of human behavior (Table 17). A ma-

Table 17.   Various Definitions of Security, or Happiness

Need	Goal
Physiological, emotional	Pursuit of sensual pleasures, wealth
Intellectual	Pursuit of knowledge, wisdom
Spiritual	Pursuit of virtue, love of God

terialistic society would define security in terms of achieving wealth and sensual satisfaction, in order to meet physiological needs. To satisfy intellectual needs, security might be interpreted as the attainment of knowledge and wisdom. Lastly, security could be regarded in spiritual terms, for instance, as the acquisition of virtue, holiness, and love of God.

It is also clear that one's conception of the nature of ultimate security is related to success in attaining it. In view of the disagreements about what should constitute man's final and supreme endeavor, how is the solution to be attained?

CRITERIA OF ULTIMATE SECURITY

There would appear to be three criteria that reveal the nature of ultimate security, or complete happiness (Table 18). Man's supreme goal should (a) completely satisfy his entire nature, including physiological, emotional, intellectual, and spiritual needs; (b) possess finality, i.e., be ultimate in itself, not sought as a means toward any further goal, and (c) be perpetual, eternal, and everlasting, and thus preclude loss.

A moment's reflection will indicate that absence of any one of these requirements would deprive man of absolute security and perfect happiness. First, man must satisfy his primary drives (e.g., hunger, thirst) in order to

Table 18. Criteria of Ultimate Security or Happiness

Criteria	Fulfillment
1. Should satisfy man's entire nature (self-actualization)	Physiological and emotional needs
	Intellectual needs
	Spiritual needs
2. Should possess finality	Terminate goal-seeking
3. Should be perpetual, eternal	Preclude loss

be content on the physiological level. Intellectually, he must acquire information to satisfy his search for wisdom and knowledge. On the spiritual level, man needs to relate to God. If it is not the Christian God, it will be one of his own making, such as the god of science or of materialism. It should be evident, then, that whatever constitutes complete happiness must completely fulfill the needs of human nature. Perhaps the psychological term most closely describing this necessity is *self-actualization* (Hall and Lindzey, 1957).

A second requisite of ultimate happiness and security is that of finality. For example, wealth as a goal is an interim rather than a final objective, for its purpose is to achieve further, specific goals. Interim objectives are wanting in respect to finality and are but temporarily satisfying. Ultimate security and happiness must terminate further seeking, and fulfill man's yearning once and for all.

Lastly, ultimate happiness must be eternal; the apprehension of possible loss would diminish the joy of any temporary possession. Absolute security exists only in the absence of fear of loss.

SECURITY IN THIS LIFE

The three criteria for absolute security can now be applied to the various kinds of happiness possessed in this life. Fulfillment of physiological and emotional needs such as hunger, thirst, or sex do not constitute complete happiness, principally because they embrace only self-love. No person is happy alone. He has a need, both emotional and intellectual, to love someone other than himself. However, such fulfillment, whether expressed in love of a person or of knowledge, is yet insufficient. Man has a need for spiritual happiness, or peace with God. A guilty conscience does not find relief in fornication, gluttony, or inebriation. Desire for peace of mind and spiritual contentment is quenched only from a spiritual reservoir.

It is also evident that, no matter what goals are attained in this life, there is still the attraction of further conquests, a restlessness incapable of being satiated. Man adapts to what he possesses, and continually seeks other ends. There is no termination of longing.

Lastly, there is the third requirement of perpetual possession. Earthly existence contains but fleeting moments of happiness, sobered always with the knowledge that they will end. A final conclusion is therefore apparent—absolute security and perfect happiness is not to be found in this life.

IMPLICATIONS AND ALTERNATIVES

What, then, are the implications? Two alternatives are possible. The first is that man possesses a basic human striving that will never be fulfilled, and that consequently he is to be forever frustrated in the quest for complete happiness and absolute security. The second alternative is that this search is to be fulfilled, but not in this temporal earthly existence. Because the first possibility leads to fatalistic despair should not be the reason for accepting the second. There is, however, positive evidence to support the second position. This evidence consists of divine revelation.

FAITH AND REASON

The choice between the two alternatives of atheistic fatalism and Christian hope rests on the presence of, or upon the lack of, faith in divine revelation. Even non-Christians who believe in a life hereafter base their conviction on faith. The reason is simple. The reality of life after death is beyond human experience, and therefore beyond human verification. Faith supplements reason, continuing from the point at which reason leaves off. Faith must, however, be reasonable, that is, must not contradict reason or be illogical. The possibility of fulfillment beyond death is reasonable, in that it is consonant with the basic human striving for absolute security and perfect happiness. The verification of this possibility, however, is beyond the realm of philosophy, and this approach in the analysis of man's ultimate goal hereby comes to a close. The theological evaluation of this problem, in terms of divine revelation, will be presented in the last chapters of this book.

Chapter 8

Determinism and Human Freedom

Human freedom is assumed by the layman to be a fact. It is also considered so precious a human attribute that forms of government are based
upon it, wars are fought for it, and monuments dedicated to it.

Contemporary psychologists, however, have protested against what they
call the myth of human freedom (R. H. Turner, 1966; Immergluck, 1964).
Freedom is an illusion, it is contended, a superstition of the past, today
exposed as such by the light of modern science. Consequently, there has
resulted the opposition between the view that man does possess freedom of
choice (voluntarism) and the view that he does not (determinism).

IMPLICATIONS OF DETERMINISM

Does this controversy have practical implications, or is it merely vague,
speculative argument? Let determinism for the moment be assumed valid.
Would incarceration of criminals be just? Certainly not. Even though the
determinist would consider punishment to be a useful corrective procedure
to redirect human behavior, the question of justice remains. Is justice, then,
also an invalid concept? To be consistent, the determinist would answer
in the affirmative.

Not only is human justice involved, but divine justice as well. The Ten Commandments imply freedom to choose between good and evil, as do divine reward and punishment. Determinism, if correct, makes of divine justice a mockery, and portrays God as fiendish rather than benevolent. It would indeed be true, if a man were unable to reject evil, that consequent condemnation to eternal perdition would be a monstrous act.

It should be obvious, therefore, that the validity or invalidity of human freedom has realistic, practical implications. It is not just a speculative or hypothetical problem; the matter requires resolution (Berofsky, 1966).

LINGUISTIC ANALYSIS AND BEHAVIORAL FREEDOM

The linguistic analyst sees the solution of the freedom-determinism controversy in describing behavior in diverse languages, descriptions that present different aspects unrelated to one another (Barbour, 1966). Thus man can be both determined and free in the same behavioral act, dependent on whether he is described in terms of spectator-language (determinism) or actor-language (voluntarism). However, this is an evasion of the issue. The preference of a scientist to use spectator-language and the preference of a philosopher to use actor-language have nothing at all to do with the objective, ontological nature of the act. In terms of reality, a behavioral act cannot be both free and nonfree (determined) in the one and same instance. The act is independent of any descriptive language. A particular behavioral act is free or not free, not both. Which alternative is true depends on the evidence intrinsic to the act itself. This evidence will be forthcoming.

WHAT FREEDOM IS AND IS NOT

Freedom refers to choice behavior. Given alternatives among which to choose, can man select without being determined by forces from within or without? Freedom is expressed in everyday language as deliberate intention ("I will"), as contrasted to action merely referred to the future ("I shall"). The question, therefore, is whether or not human choice behavior can be free rather than determined.

Freedom in behavior does not mean absence of causality. The voluntarist does not contend that human behavior is uncaused, but rather that there is a cause (the self) operating in a free manner to produce effects (choices). It is the relationship between cause and effect that is under question: Is man (cause) determined in his choice (effect), or does he produce such an effect freely?

Freedom is not variance (Boring, 1957). The statistical variability of accumulative behavioral responses, referred to as the standard deviation of a distribution, does not constitute human freedom. Animals lower than man, even the earthworm, possess behavioral variability, yet the voluntarist does not attribute freedom to such behavior. Statistical variability can be explained in terms of the imprecision of the measuring instrument, the lack of experimental control of all the variables entering into a response, and the circumstances changing from one measured situation to the next. Human freedom can induce variability, but the presence of variability does not necessarily imply freedom.

APPROACHES TO THE PROBLEM

How is the voluntarism-determinism controversy to be approached? Can the experimental method yield a solution? Consider for a moment a person's choice between red and green color cards. His instructions are to choose but one color. After a few seconds of thought the subject selects green. Was his choice free, or was it determined by previous positive and negative associations with colors, or possibly by his present emotional mood, or by the laboratory surroundings? The subject's tendency to favor green might be predicted from previous knowledge of such antecedent variables, but does this mean he was predetermined, or even presently determined, to choose green? The experimental method cannot answer this question, nor should it be expected to. The experimental method can indicate the choice made, but must remain silent concerning the relationship of the chooser to his decision.

Next, there is the theological method. Contingent on one's theological frame of reference (for there is a form of theological determinism, as will be seen), it could be inferred from the Ten Commandments that man is capable of choosing freely between moral good and moral evil. The concept of God as being essentially good and just and the concept of divine reward and punishment necessarily imply human freedom. But theological truths are not readily apparent, nor are they universally acceptable to all men. There is, however, a third approach to the problem, and that is the rational method of philosophy. The voluntarist contends that freedom can be inferred from a reasonable analysis of observed data.

EVIDENCE FOR VOLUNTARISM

There are three types of evidence for human freedom (Table 19). The first is the *capacity for voluntary attention*. Attention is the act of directing the focal point of awareness to some object. At this moment, the reader's attention is upon this page. Since this behavior is deliberate, the reader's state of attention is called voluntary. If, however, a sudden noise were to draw this attention aside, the interruption would illustrate involuntary attention. The fundamental awareness that attention is at times under personal control and, in other instances, is not demonstrates human freedom. If this were not so, there would be no awareness at all of the difference between these two states of mind. It should also be noted here that attention is defined in terms of awareness, not in other referent terms such as posture, set, or physiological threshold (Woodworth and Schlosberg, 1954).

A second confirmation of human freedom stems from the nature of *conscience*. The same act can be perceived differently, contingent on the awareness of guilt. When a motorist unexpectedly strikes a child, the incident is acknowledged to be accidental. To run down a pedestrian deliberately, however, clearly involves personal responsibility. The experience of guilt in the second instance would illustrate the action of conscience and is indicative of the fundamental awareness that in the area of moral behavior one can commit evil acts that need not have been done or could have been freely avoided. The experience of guilt is so universal that persons lacking such awareness are classified as psychopathic (Coleman, 1964).

The third verification of human freedom comes from *pride of accomplishment*. The college student, the carpenter apprentice, the reformed alcoholic—all pursue goals freely chosen and experience pride in their achievement. The human reaction involved in working toward an achieved goal is different from that experienced in winning a prize without effort. The difference is that in one instance freedom plays the important role, while in the other it is good fortune.

Table 19. Attributes of Freedom

Evidence for freedom:	1.	Capacity for voluntary attention
	2.	Conscience
	3.	Pride of achievement
Prerequisites for freedom:	1.	Awareness
	2.	Deliberation

PREREQUISITES FOR FREEDOM

It is also evident that all human behavior is not free. There are certain prerequisite conditions (Table 19). The first condition is *awareness*. An individual must be aware that a decision or choice is being made. Putting the wrong end of a cigarette in the mouth is illustrative of the absence of awareness, and such preoccupied acts are not free. Other examples might be brushing away a fly or scratching an itch. Spontaneous or automatic habitual acts conducted below the level of awareness are not free.

The second condition necessary for a free act is *deliberation*. The person must have opportunity to consider choices of action prior to decision. The time factor in this reflection will vary with person and circumstances. A few seconds may be adequate at times, whereas complex decisions may require hours. The condition of deliberation, incidentally, enters into judgment of a murderer. There are several legally defined degrees of murder, contingent on the amount of forethought of the accused, although the victim has been equally disposed of in all instances.

When awareness and deliberation are lacking, either in degree or in entirety, there is corresponding attenuation of freedom and responsibility. For example, an anger response to personal insult may be so immediate as to preclude any decision for emotional control. This first reaction, therefore, is not free. The consequent decision to permit the emotional state to continue, however, is free. There are many such normal impulses that are not initially free. In the area of moral behavior, for example, they are considered to be *temptations*, and, lacking the element of freedom, are thereby distinguished from *sin*, the consequent acceptance of a temptation. In summary, spontaneous impulses, whether due to emotion or past habit, are not free acts; it is upon subsequent reflection and the decision to accept or reject the impulse that freedom enters. These necessary prerequisite conditions for freedom in behavior are also helpful in determining the presence or absence of responsibility in the psychotic and in the mentally deficient. They are also relevant to the analysis of freedom in cases of coercion by physical and mental torture leading to the breakdown of normal intellectual functioning.

Next will be examined ten contemporary theories of determinism, all objecting to the voluntarist's position (Table 20).

Table 20.   Ten Theories of Determinism

(1).	Skeptic determinism
(2).	Mechanistic determinism
(3).	Biological or genetic determinism
(4).	Stimulus-response determinism
(5).	Reinforcement determinism
(6).	Socioeconomic and cultural determinism
(7).	Motivational determinism
(8).	Psychoanalytic determinism
(9).	Creationistic determinism
(10).	Omniscient determinism

SKEPTIC DETERMINISM

The common basis for testimony of freedom is awareness, or the consciousness of this capability. Skeptic determinism strikes at the root of this conviction by asserting consciousness to be an invalid informational source. For example, an amputee may attribute sensation to a foot no longer present; a straight stick placed partly in water appears bent. In both instances the skeptic contends that consciousness has lied.

However, the opposite is true; consciousness is a valid source of information. Past learning accounts for the discrepancy between fact and judgment in the first example. A person learns to refer sensation to different parts of the body. Stimulation of a nerve path anywhere along its length will be spatially localized in accordance with associated stimuli learned throughout life. The amputee, experiencing a sensation at the end of the leg stump, will, because of previous learning, refer this sensation to the foot, even though that foot is now missing.

With regard to the bent-stick illusion, advantage has been taken of the structure of the human eye, which does not naturally correct for refraction of light in two media. A judgment is made on an abnormal situation—the stick appears bent and is so judged. Nor should the eye be expected to operate outside its normal setting, any more so than it should be expected to read license plates on cars whizzing by at two hundred miles per hour.

The skeptic, therefore, attempts to use abnormal settings to discredit the testimony of consciousness in normal circumstances. A similar argument would be that if a blind man cannot see, no man can.

A more critical reply to the skeptic, however, concerns the validity of his own positiveness. Can he doubt the trustworthiness of consciousness while using that consciousness as a basis for his doubt? Obviously not. The skeptic, in removing the basis for the validity of any doubt, consequently discredits his own. He therefore cannot make any firm positive statement on the matter. He can only hold to a doubt that in itself is doubtful.

To the voluntarist, the skeptic position only points out the remarkable capability of the human mind to pose two kinds of doubts—those that are reasonable and those that are not. To doubt consciousness is unreasonable, and such doubts are unworthy of retention.

MECHANISTIC DETERMINISM

If man is a machine, then it follows that he, like other machines, is controlled by outside forces, and therefore his behavior is determined.

The voluntarist replies with the vitalistic opposition to mechanism, previously discussed. Because living things are essentially distinct from nonliving things and machines, human freedom is possible. That man does possess such freedom has been demonstrated.

BIOLOGICAL OR GENETIC DETERMINISM

Adherents of biological determinism are prevalent in the biological sciences. Heredity, temperament, glands, and emotions are supposedly the architects of the human personality and the dictators of action.

It is admissible that the feebleminded person and the organic psychotic are individuals lacking freedom to a great extent, or possibly completely. The absence of the facility of deliberation, a necessary prerequisite to free choice, explains the limited freedom in such instances. However, here again factors present in abnormal situations are not arguments against freedom in normal circumstances. Because some men are blind does not mean no man can see.

As for extreme emotional states, it is again admissible that freedom can be attenuated. However, in the initial stages of emotional buildup, e.g., sexual arousal, a free resolve can be made to curb the response or to permit its continuance. Similarly with cases of alcoholism and drug addiction. In the beginning the decision to permit the behavior pattern is freely formed. It is only consequent to this decision, as the habit is continued, that a possible irrevocable pattern becomes established.

In conclusion, therefore, man freely decides whether or not initial impulses are to be followed. While inherited emotional temperament may influence behavior, it does not always control or compel behavior.

STIMULUS-RESPONSE DETERMINISM

A fourth theory of determinism, stimulus-response determinism, is held by certain learning theorists. The conditioned response will illustrate. A puff of air directed at the eye will cause the eye to blink reflexively. Repetition of this procedure, accompanied by a buzzer sounded simultaneously with the air puff, will eventually result in the eye's blinking at the sound of the buzzer in the absence of the air puff. This simple example of conditioned behavior is sometimes used to arrive at the sweeping generalization that all human behavior is likewise conditioned and that, consequently, freedom is precluded.

The voluntarist points out the lack of evidence for this generalization. It is true that reflex conditioning can occur in human learning, even below the threshold of awareness, as in the conditioned pupillary reflex. However, man exhibits more than one type of learning process. Some learning patterns require concentrated effort, as in the case of learning to play golf or in mastering algebra. The attempt to reduce all human learning to simple conditioning is arbitrary and unwarranted.

REINFORCEMENT DETERMINISM

A theory closely resembling stimulus-response determinism, but broader in concept, is that of educational determinism, or reinforcement determinism, which introduces the role of reward and punishment as factors that shape behavior. As E. L. Thorndike originally described the situation, rewarded behavior is stamped in the person, and punished behavior is stamped out.

Subsequent theorists have replaced the term *reward* with that of *reinforcement*. Whatever reinforces behavior determines its repetition. However, the fact that reinforced behavior is repeated does not necessarily imply a determined relationship. The human subject merely observes that rewarded behavior is a more pleasant experience than unrewarded behavior and consequently chooses the former alternative. Such a choice is obviously the logical one to make. Furthermore, such experiments only indicate the course of action chosen, and shed no light on whether or not the choice was free or determined.

SOCIOECONOMIC AND CULTURAL DETERMINISM

Socioeconomic determinism is the view that behavior is shaped by socioeconomic forces such as home, school, church, and community. These environmental variables indoctrinate the individual and structure his choice behavior. For example, slums are said to breed criminals.

The voluntarist considers social forces to be influences rather than determining causes. Good citizens can develop within conditions of poverty, and criminal delinquents can emerge from high socioeconomic levels. Freedom can certainly be attenuated in an individual suffering the stresses of poverty, but freedom need not be completely eradicated. Certainly the number of choices is limited; his choice is between a one-dollar or two-dollar item, rather than between a five-dollar or ten-dollar item. Again, the person exercising choice between work as a ditchdigger or as a farmhand is no less free than the person deciding between an engineering career or one of law. Although socioeconomic factors certainly determine the kind and number of opportunities available, choice *among* the offered alternatives is nonetheless free.

Cultural determinism is a broader development of the socioeconomic position. Here culture is proposed as the determiner of behavior. The existence of stereotypes such as the "typical" Frenchman or Britisher is indicative of a common mold peculiar to individual societies. Culture indeed impresses attitudes, values, and interests upon its members.

It can therefore be granted that modes of behavior differ from one culture to another. These are expressed in language, fashion, and outlook. The Britisher may enjoy tea, whereas the American prefers coffee, and the Frenchman wine. While the African engages in a lion hunt, the Scotsman pursues quail. It is obvious, then, that *kinds* of behavior are dictated by culture, and perhaps equally well by geography. However, freedom is not concerned with the nature of alternative causes of action, but rather the choice among such modes. The cognitive processes involved in the choice between fishing and golf are no different from those employed in the decision of whether to ski or to bobsled. Decision-making behavior is a human activity as natural and universal as walking or sleeping. Man, in spite of the culture in which he finds himself, intellectually chooses freely *among* offered alternative courses of action.

MOTIVATIONAL DETERMINISM

A seventh objection to the concept of human freedom is that of motivational determinism, expressed by the statement, the stronger motive prevails. If one decides to attend a movie rather than a concert, it is supposedly because the movie holds greater attraction and determining force than the concert (Lewin, 1935).

The fault in motivational determinism is akin to that of the Monday-morning quarterback. The "prevailing" motive is not labeled until after the decision is made. Thus, no matter what alternative is selected, the determinist would obligingly designate it as the stronger one. To do so proves nothing. The knowledge that a decision has been made gives no information on whether or not there was freedom or lack of freedom existing prior to the decision. Liberty prior to choice must be settled by other considerations, and these have already been discussed.

Another example offered by motivational determinists is that of *reactive inhibition* (Hull, 1943). It can be predicted that a subject, after having pressed a red-light button for a hundred trials and then having been given the opportunity to push a light button other than red, will usually select the alternative. Behavioral reactive inhibition induced by the hundred trials determines the selection of an alternative choice, contends the determinist. The voluntarist replies that certainly the tendency to change behavior is present, but the impulse need not be followed. The reader may have recognized reactive inhibition as an equivalent term for monotony. A repetitive behavior pattern will usually induce the impulse or tendency to alternative activity, a response natural to life forms, which, in man, may even be consciously experienced. However, the person is still free to follow or to reject the impulse. Tendencies are not behavioral determinants, but rather behavioral influences.

PSYCHOANALYTIC DETERMINISM

An eighth objection to the proposed existence of human freedom is that of psychoanalysis, which stresses the role of the unconscious in the determination of behavior. The unconscious harbors primitive instincts and forgotten or repressed memories—fears, desires, and so on—which may direct behavior without one's being aware of it (Freud, 1943). For example, a mother may find fault with her daughter's suitors because of an unconscious desire to retain her child's affections. The convenient headache that develops appropriately to excuse one from unpleasant obligations may be unconsciously motivated. Psychoanalysts, on the evidence of unconscious defense mechanisms, deny freedom of choice. Even though on the conscious level man is convinced of such freedom, it is contended that there are unconscious forces, unknown to the individual, manipulating the decision-making process.

This operation of unconscious variables can be illustrated by the iceberg paradigm (Figure 9). The visible part of an iceberg is no index of the shape of that part submerged beneath the water's surface. Two icebergs of apparently equal visual size above the water level need not have the same configuration below the water level. Analogously, the apparent equivalence of two conscious or "visible" choices is actually in error, since they differ in their unconscious or "invisible" components. Therefore, it is the alternative with the greater unconscious component that will ultimately determine the decision.

The fault with this line of reasoning is that the unconscious, being unconscious, is unknowable. The voluntarist, by the same token, could argue that the unconscious force of the rejected alternative was actually the stronger, and the chooser exerted great effort in his decision to overcome it. Since the role of motivation below the level of awareness is an unknowable variable, it is purely arbitrary to assign various strengths of influence to one alternative or another. Unconscious motivation cannot, therefore, be

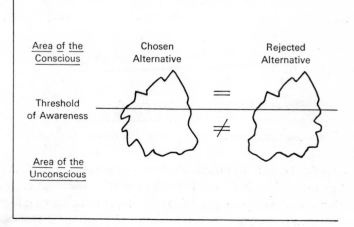

FIG. 9. Psychoanalytic Determinism.

used to prove or disprove freedom of choice. Only positive evidence above
the threshold of awareness can be cited. Such evidence indicates that man
is free.

A ninth deterministic theory is encountered in theology. Creationistic
determinism is based on the Law of Causality, which states that effects are
utterly dependent on their causes. If so, it follows that man, as an effect
created by God, his cause, would be completely dependent upon the Creator in all human activity, including decision behavior. Man is consequently
a divinely manipulated puppet. The idea that God predestines certain souls
to heaven and others to hell is related to creationistic determinism.

The fallacy of this viewpoint is the unnecessary extrapolation of a law in
the physical world to the world of the spiritual. In the material cosmos it is
true that effects are completely dependent upon and determined by their
causes. But is it not possible that different cause-effect relations exist on the
nonmaterial, or spiritual, level? God could, if he so desired, create a being
with free will, dependent upon him for existence, but nonetheless possessing the capacity for freedom of choice. In no way would this concept do
violence to the laws governing the material universe. Freedom exists as an
immaterial, or spiritual, behavior pattern, since such activity is a function
of the mind, itself immaterial. (The immaterial nature of mind has been
discussed in Chapter 5.) This possibility that God created man as a free
creature is positively confirmed by evidence available, already cited.

The tenth and last theory of determinism is also found in theology.
Since God is omniscient (all-knowing), he knows man's choice before it is
made. Consequently it would appear that his knowledge determines that
choice.

It is true that God knows the entire lifetime of every individual, even prior
to that person's birth. Does such knowledge thereby determine behavior?
The voluntarist replies with an analogy. A person having seen a football
game, and then reviewing it on film, could predict during the film exactly
what the players would do next. If he were not bound by time, he could also

have predicted the play at the time of watching the game. In neither instance would such knowledge be the cause of the players' reactions. By analogy, God, not being bound by time, knows while the game is being played what will happen. All things are present to God. This attribute, that of omniscience, is lacking in man, who must live out each moment of time and know the future only as it becomes the present. Therefore, it should be apparent that knowledge of behavior, even God's knowledge, is not the cause of that behavior. God could, of course, if he so desired, control human activities completely. The question here is not whether or not God possesses this power; it is rather whether or not his knowledge alone predetermines human choice. That it need not has been demonstrated. That it *does* not is verified by the logical evidence for freedom, as well as by the Ten Commandments, which presume personal freedom.

CONCLUSION

The evidence for freedom of choice, and the necessary prerequisite conditions, have been presented. Ten theories objecting to the claims for this human capability have been examined, and each has been found wanting. In conclusion, it may be stated that man is *self-determining* in his behavior (Arnold and Gasson, 1954). Within him lies a sovereign right to choose freely among offered alternatives, to direct, control, and accomplish personal objectives. Whether or not the reader agrees with the evidence ... rests on a free decision.

PART II   SUGGESTED READINGS

Adler, M. J. *The difference of man and the difference it makes.* New York: World (Meridian paperback), 1968. Ch. 3. "The State of the Question, Past, Present, and Future;" Ch. 7. "The Laboratory Findings and Their Interpretation," Part III. "The Difference it Makes."

Allport, G. W. *The person in psychology.* Boston: Beacon Press, 1968. Part I. "Which Model for the Person?"

Allport, G. W. *Pattern and growth in personality.* New York: Holt, Rinehart, and

Winston, 1961. Ch. 2. "Personality, Character, Temperament"; Ch. 5. "Principles of Learning"; Ch. 6. "The Evolving Sense of Self"; Ch. 22. "The Person in Psychology."

Arnold, M., & Gasson, J. *The human person.* New York: Ronald, 1954. Ch. 1. "Basic Assumptions in Psychology" (Arnold).

Barbour, I. The significance of Teilhard. *The Christian Century,* 1967, *84,* 1090–1102.

Barbour, I. G. *Issues in science and religion.* Englewood Cliffs: Prentice-Hall, 1966. Ch. 10. "Physics and Indeterminacy; Ch. 11. "Life and Mind"; Ch. 12. "Evolution and Creation."

Barbour, I. *Christianity and the scientist.* New York: Association Press, 1960. Ch. 1. "Introduction: The Vocation of the Scientist."

Berofsky, B. *Free will and determinism.* New York: Harper & Row, 1966. Ch. 1. "Determinism"; Ch. 3. "Libertarianism."

Bertalanffy, L. von. *General systems theory: Essays on its foundation and development.* New York: Braziller, 1968. Ch. 10. "The Relativity of Categories."

Bertalanffy, L. von. *Robots, men, and minds: Psychology in the modern world.* New York: Braziller, 1967. Part II. "Toward a New Natural Philosophy."

Bittle, C. N. *The whole man.* Milwaukee: Bruce, 1945. Ch. XVI. "Freedom of Will"; Ch. XIX. "The Vital Principle"; Ch. XVI. "The Human Person"; Ch. XXIII. "The Destiny of Man."

Bugental, J. F. T. *Challenges of humanistic psychology.* New York: McGraw-Hill, 1967. Ch. 29. "Self-Actualization and Beyond" (Maslow); Ch. 34. "The World of Science and the World of Value" (Bertalanffy).

Cofer, C. N., and Appley, M. H. *Motivation: Theory and research.* New York: Wiley, 1964. Ch. 13. "Self-Actualization and Related Concepts."

Donceel, J. F. *Philosophical psychology* (2d Ed.). New York: Sheed & Ward, 1965. Part I: "Life in General"; Ch. 17. "The Human Will"; Ch. 19. "Man's Soul and Body"; Appendix; "Theology and Evolution."

du Noüy, L. *Human destiny.* New York: Longmans, Greene, 1947. Ch. 8. "The New Orientation of Evolution: Man. The Second Chapter of Genesis."

Francoeur, R. T. *Perspectives in evolution.* Baltimore: Helicon, 1965. Ch. 3. "Scientific Evolution"; Ch. 4. "The Ascending Spiral."

Hook, S. (Ed.) *Dimensions of mind.* New York: New York University Press, 1959. Ch. 2. "Mind-Body, Not a Pseudoproblem" (Feigl): Ch. 8. "In Defense of Dualism" (Ducasse).

Hook, S. (Ed.) *Determinism and freedom.* New York: New York University Press, 1957. Part I, Ch. 3. "Determinism and Novelty" (Barrett); Part IV, Ch. 16. "Common Sense and Beyond" (Weiss).

Lawrence, N., and O'Connor, D. *Readings in existential phenomenology.* Englewood Cliffs: Prentice-Hall, 1967. Ch. 13. "Freedom and Responsibility" (Wild).

Lindzey, G., and Hall, C. S. *Theories of personality: Primary sources and research.* New York: Wiley, 1965. Section VI, Ch. 1. "The Open System in Personality

Theory" (Allport); Section VII, Ch. 4. "Some Basic Propositions of a Growth and Self-Actualization Psychology" (Maslow).

Madsen, K. B. *Theories of motivation.* Cleveland: Howard Allen, 1961. Ch. 2. "Scientific Theories"; Ch. 17. "Comparison of the Structure of the Theories."

Matson, F. W. *The broken image: Man, science, and society.* New York: Braziller, 1964. Ch. IV. "An Uncertain Trumpet: The New Physics"; Ch. V. "The Ambiguity of Life: The Biology of Freedom"; Ch. VI. "The Freedom to Be Human: New Directions in Psychology."

May, R. *Psychology and the human dilemma.* Princeton: van Nostrand, 1967. Part Four. "Freedom and Responsibility."

Misiak, H., and Sexton, V. *History of psychology.* New York: Grune & Stratton, 1966. Ch. 3. "Psychological Thought in Modern Philosophy."

Moore, R. *Evolution.* (Life Nature Library). New York: Time, Life, 1964. Ch. 4. "Chromosomes, Genes, and DNA."

Moore, T. V. *The driving forces of human nature and their adjustment.* New York: Grune & Stratton, 1948. Ch. 28. "The Philosophy of Will."

Royce, J. E. *Man and meaning.* New York: McGraw-Hill, 1969. Part IV. "The Whole Person."

Royce, J. R. (Ed.) *Psychology and the symbol.* New York: Random House, 1965. Ch. 2. "On the Definition of the Symbol" (Bertalanffy).

Sahakian, W. S. *Psychology of personality: Readings in theory.* Chicago: Rand McNally, 1965. Ch. 4. "Humanistic Psychoanalysis" (Fromm); Ch. 14. "Self-Actualization" (Maslow); Ch. 20. "The Phenomenological Theory of Personality" (Rogers).

Severin, F. T. *Humanistic viewpoints in psychology.* New York: McGraw-Hill, 1965. Ch. 5. "Conflicting Views of Man's Basic Nature" (Coleman); Ch. 6. "The Unconscious and Freedom" (Nuttin); Ch. 7. "On Choice and Responsibility in a Humanistic Psychotherapy" (Temerlin).

Sutich, A., and Vich, M. (Eds.) *Readings in humanistic psychology.* New York: The Free Press, 1969. Ch. 1. "Toward a Science of the Person" (Rogers).

Teilhard de Chardin, P. *The phenomenon of man.* New York: Harper & Row, 1959. Book Three, Ch. 1. "The Birth of Thought"; Ch. 3. "The Modern Earth"; Book Four: "Survival."

Van der Veldt, J. H., and Odenwald, R. P. *Psychiatry and Catholicism.* New York: McGraw-Hill, 1952. Ch. 1. "Person and Personality."

PART III

HUMAN ADJUSTMENT

A next logical step, after studying basic evaluative methods in psychology (Part I) and their application to the study of human nature (Part II), is the examination of personal adjustment, in terms of interaction with environment.

Chapter 9 discusses the roots of guilt and anxiety in contemporary society. In Chapter 10 the criteria of healthy adjustment are presented, with an analysis of physical, intellectual, social, and moral maturity. Emotional adjustment is examined in Chapter 11, with respect to cultivating healthy emotional growth in the child, the adolescent, and the adult.

Chapter 9

Contemporary Anxiety

The present era has been characterized as "The Age of Anxiety." Uncertainty and fear exist on the international level, within nations, and within individuals. Consider for a moment the state of adjustment, or rather, maladjustment, of contemporary American society. As was noted earlier, half of the hospital beds in the United States are occupied by mental patients, and it is estimated that one of every twelve Americans will spend part of his life in a mental institution (Coleman, 1969). State hospitals cannot meet the flow of incoming psychiatric patients. The average state mental hospital has but sixty percent of the number of psychiatrists, twenty-five percent of the psychologists, and thirty percent of the nurses needed for efficient operation.

Antisocial behavior can also be considered an index of a nation's state of adjustment. According to annual crime reports of the FBI, the crime rate has been increasing six times faster than the population growth. And a great percentage of arrests are of teenagers. Finally, the stability of the home is a good indicator of adjustment. In the United States one of every four marriages ends in divorce, with serious consequences for the mental health of tomorrow's generation.

FEAR, ANXIETY, AND GUILT

Before examining the causes of anxiety in our present time, it would be well to define the concept. Anxiety should be further distinguished from fear and guilt, and differences between normal and abnormal aspects of these states recognized.

Fear can be defined as the reaction to a specific, known threat, such as a sudden confrontation with a wild animal. The cause of the fear reaction is clearly perceived by the endangered person. Anxiety, on the other hand, is less differentiated and more diffuse. In fact, the cause of the reaction is unknown to the person experiencing it. There is only the feeling that personal existence is being threatened, physically or psychologically, in terms of one's self-concept and value system. Anxiety is consequently referred to as "free-floating," unanchored to a specific fear stimulus (May, 1950). Physical symptoms of anxiety include palpitation of the heart, breathing difficulty, and gastrointestinal upset. Psychologically, the feeling of impending doom can be expressed as anticipated threat, similar to apprehension of an auto collision when approaching an intersection. Or again, there may be a jumpy feeling or exaggerated startle reaction to any sudden stimulus.

Figure 10 presents the various stages in the development of anxiety. A threatening experience is followed by the unconscious attempt to forget (repression). However, even though the situation causing the fear may be successfully relegated to the unconscious, the fear response, if the threat is in continuing status, will eventually force its way into consciousness. Since the cause is still unknown to the subject, the resultant experience is a free-

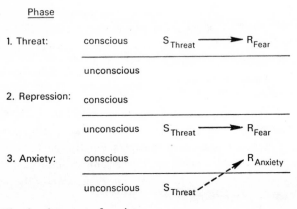

FIG. 10.   The development of anxiety.

floating, unanchored anxiety. Usually anxiety is intolerable, and the subject frequently attaches the anxiety response to a stimulus other than the real cause. For example, a relative of the author once suffered mild but continuing anxiety which she attached to a fear of a possible nuclear war. However, the anxiety state terminated when her husband obtained a different position. Further questioning revealed that the husband in his former work traveled frequently on commercial airlines, and, at the time, several airline disasters had been front-page news. The woman's anxiety was really caused by the possibility that her husband would be killed in a plane accident. Consciously knowing, however, that his work necessitated air travel, she had repressed this fear. The consequent emergence of an anxiety response on the conscious level was then attached to something which in actuality held less threat for her, that of a nuclear emergency. This case not only illustrates the genesis of anxiety, but also the occasional attempt to attribute the response to an acceptable stimulus that holds no real threat.

Guilt, always perceived as threatening, follows a pattern similar to that of fear repression.

NORMAL AND NEUROTIC REACTIONS

Rollo May, in a classical treatment of anxiety (1950), distinguishes normal from neurotic anxiety. Neurotic anxiety is (a) disproportionate to the objective danger, (b) involves serious repression, and (c) is managed by neurotic mechanisms. Normal anxiety, on the other hand, lacks these characteristics.

A similar distinction exists between normal and neurotic guilt (Schneiders, 1965). Guilt may be defined as the awareness of having done something deserving punishment. Neurotic guilt is (a) disproportionate to the wrong committed, (b) may induce repression, and (c) is often accompanied by neurotic anxiety. Normal guilt, however, involves full awareness of the moral transgression, the acknowledgement of responsibility, and the realization that amends are in order. Repression may occur if the guilt state continues.

ANXIETY, HOSTILITY, AND REPRESSION

The unfortunate consequence of anxiety is the vicious circle to which it may lead—anxiety, hostility, repression, and more anxiety (May, 1950). The sequence of these events is presented in Figure 11.

Unresolved frustration or conflict, perceived as threatening, will eventually be repressed. For the child, parental displeasure or discipline may evoke a feeling of alienation. Since the parent is the child's source of affection, love, and security, deprivation of these factors induces anxiety. On the adult level, rejection by one's employer, for example, may evoke similar feelings. The anxiety state introduces hostility, in accordance with the well-validated "frustration-aggression" hypothesis (Miller et al., 1941). The child feels resentment against parents, and the adult experiences antagonism toward (a) those who have placed him in the present situation, (b) those who in the past (parents) have not prepared him to cope with present conflict, and (c) himself, for lacking adequately adjustive responses. There is also the impulse to displace this aggression toward neutral persons or objects.

The next step is repression of the anxiety and hostility experienced. The child, fearing further parental reprisal, as well as further alienation of affection, may repress any display of hostility. Reasons for repression of hostility by the adult would include fear of engendering further rejection by significant persons involved, and the dim awareness of the possibility that oneself is to blame, not another. Repression of the anxiety state occurs because anxiety itself is perceived as threatening. The final consequence, completing the circle, is induction of further anxiety. Repression induces anxiety because (a) repression permits contradictions between conscious and unconscious beliefs, (b) repression renders the individual less able to distinguish and cope with dangers, and (c) repressed anxiety and hostility tend to break through the repressor mechanism and force their way into consciousness.

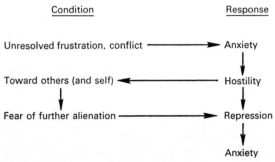

FIG. 11.   Relation of anxiety, hostility, and repression.

The vicious circle of anxiety, hostility, and repression may be entered at any point and may also follow different sequential patterns.

The paradigm of human reaction to guilt is similar to that for anxiety.

ANXIETY AND ECONOMIC EVOLUTION

May (1950) has presented an excellent analysis of the psychological and cultural origins of anxiety. The following material partially embraces his viewpoint, supplemented by the author's considerations.

May cites a work by Tawney (1920) on the relation of cultural development to the genesis of anxiety. During the Renaissance, man broke away from the security of group identity and membership and found himself alone. Competition, rather than cooperation, became the motivating factor in success. Economic individualism emerged more freely in the nineteenth century, in the personal struggle for power. Work and craftsmanship lost their intrinsic value, and wealth, rather than being the means of acquiring ends, became an and in itself. Unfortunately, however, the possession of wealth is relative. Consequently, one feels the compulsion to do better than one's neighbors, and failure engenders anxiety. This anxiety is further increased by a confusion between freedom and realization. A democratic society provides freedom for the individual to seek wealth, but success for

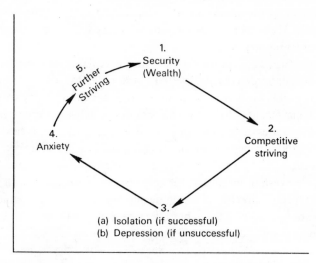

FIG. 12. Anxiety consequent to competitive striving for wealth.

all is impossible. Furthermore, competition in itself leads to anxiety, because of its concomitant isolation. Therefore, success *or* failure in competitive striving for wealth leads to anxiety and a subsequent vicious circle (Figure 12).

ANXIETY AND RESPONSIBILITY

Fromm (1941) points out the double aspect of human freedom. Positively speaking, man is free to determine his social order, but this prerogative involves the assumption of personal responsibility, which can be negatively perceived as a burden. Man consequently may seek release from the cares of decision-making and forfeit the social reins to a father figure, or dictator. Fromm thus explains the rise of Hitler in Nazi Germany, and he entitled his work on this subject *Escape from Freedom*.

ANXIETY AND MATERIALISM

A primary source of anxiety is the present-day emphasis on materiality. The sensual side of human nature is given undue attention, to the neglect of the intellectual and spiritual. Advertising reflects this sentiment in the sale of things from deodorants to automobiles. Be good to yourself, seek pleasure, and enjoy life are fashionable slogans. The sensualistic theme in modern dance, the world of fashion, and as a way of life pervades every aspect of contemporary American society.

In 1960, renowned college mentors sounded baccalaureate alarms which are still ringing unheeded (TIME 1960). For example, Princeton University President Robert F. Goheen: "Near and far the cheap and tawdry are glorified over achievements of solid worth; opiates of half-truth are seized in preference to realities of fact and need. . . . We find ourselves as a nation on the defensive and as a people seemingly paralyzed in self-indulgence."

Harvard President Nathan M. Pusey: "To many, not just the colleges but the whole Western world has for some time seemed adrift with little sense of purposeful direction, lacking deeply held conviction, wandering along with no more stirring thought in the minds of most men than desire for diversion, personal comfort and safety."

Yale College Dean William C. DeVane: "The world that a young man enters today is a glittering and insidious thing. . . . We must acknowledge that the loss of faith in our world, our destiny, our religion, is the cloudy and dark climate which most of America finds itself living in today. The individual may do what he likes to further his own gain. The man of wealth owns a whole district of slum dwellings, and feels no pangs of conscience for the hunger, squalor and disease he encourages. The aggressive salesman makes outrageous claims for the product he wishes to sell. The novelist writes a scrofulous book in hope of being on the best-seller list, and television corrupts the public taste.... I seem to have worked myself into a most unhappy state of gloom by all this."

University of California Chancellor Samuel B. Gould: "The challenge of the hour is one in which we face adversity for the first time in our history. We face the moral and spiritual adversity within our own borders brought on by a general slackening of will, a general tendency to countenance cupidity and applaud cunning, a general distrust of intellectual pursuits and those who pursue them, each a general vagueness as to national purpose and resolve. We have learned to distrust the intangible, to fear the nonconformist, to worship the material."

ANXIETY AND SEX

The confusion between sex and love, together with the distorted emphasis on the former is a further source of anxiety today. Novels erroneously equate these two human needs. To elevate sexual satisfaction to a level higher than other and more primary drives is to unbalance human nature. The acceptance of the *Playboy* philosophy of life eventually leads to frustration, guilt, and anxiety. Why? Because man is more than just animal. All human needs can be satisfied in this life without guilt or anxiety *when* they are enjoyed in their proper perspective. Sexual enjoyment is for the married, according to Christian philosophy, and only within the married state can its proper role be understood, and only then does it lead to sanctification (see Chapter 13).

ANXIETY AND MORAL EVIL

Many modern psychologists, sociologists, anthropologists, and philosophers deny the Christian explanation of the origin of moral evil. These theorists prefer to consider sin but another form of maladjustment, and then only if guilt is induced.

It is difficult to determine whether atheistic thinkers form contemporary social values or whether they are a product of them. Be that as it may, the greatest problem facing today's religious leaders is that of convincing people that sinful behavior is evil behavior. Sin is laughed at, made light of, and even rewarded. Not infrequently, adultery on the part of a notable figure enhances that person's esteem and popularity. Immorality in films, plays, and novels is welcomed by the public, which by acclamation bestows awards and praise.

Nonetheless, the denial of sin as moral evil evokes anxiety. Why? Because every person (*a*) is born with a conscience (see Chapter 12), and (*b*) the voice of conscience, even if temporarily repressed, prevents any enduring rationalization of guilt. A further factor increasing moral anxiety is the absence of any sound excuse for moral ignorance. Two thousand years ago, Christ pointed this out clearly: "If the world hates you, know that it has hated me before you. If you were of the world, the world would love what is its own. But because you are not of the world, but I have chosen you out of the world, therefore the world hates you. . . . If I had not come and spoken to them, they would have no sin. But now they have no excuse for their sin" (John 15:18–19,22).

In the twentieth century there is ample opportunity for moral education. Continual avoidance of moral instruction is itself a cause of additional anxiety, since avoidance of any obligation evokes guilt.

Neglect of one's moral education leads also to stunted spiritual growth, and deprivation of this vital need will eventually end in great unhappiness (see Chapters 15 and 16).

ANXIETY AND TRANSITION

Another source of anxiety in today's culture is the change from emphasis on permanence to emphasis on transition. This change is evident in every phase of society. In art and architecture new fads appear regularly. In industry, appliances and machines are no longer built for endurance. In education, some teachers frequently change texts, not because of new theories or concepts, but merely for the sake of change. In entertainment, even the younger generation is hard put to keep up with the rapid change in dance styles. In the area of values, transition is also rampant. The traditional virtues of honesty, integrity, and patriotism are being questioned. Academic scandals have hit West Point, Annapolis, and the Air Force Academy, supposed citadels of what is noblest and highest in the American heritage. In the field of sports, former ideals of clean competition have been tarnished by bribery and the compromise of team allegiance.

Even the home has been contaminated by the emphasis on change. One of four marriages terminates in divorce, and the broken home is today's greatest promoter of youthful crime.

Permanence, unfortunately, has become equated with stagnation, and transition with progress. However, deep within the human spirit there lies the yearning and the need for absolute security and permanence. The neglect of the fulfillment of this need, together with the acceptance of a value system that stresses only the temporary, is a source of profound anxiety in modern man.

Chapter 10

Adjustment and Maturity

The previous chapter has indicated the sad state of affairs in which American society finds itself, with regard to mental health and adjustment. However, though an individual may be unable to change culture, he can at least find ways of coping with it.

CRITERIA OF GOOD ADJUSTMENT

Many texts in the area of mental health consider average behavior to be normal behavior, and therefore desirable behavior. An individual is considered normal on a personality test, for example, if his score approximates the mean score of his peer group. However, the statistical average is not always a good criterion of healthy personality or of healthy adjustment (Schneiders, 1965). The average six-year-old child has four or five cavities; the average smoker consumes a pack of cigarettes daily; a city of a certain population has an average crime rate. Obviously, in none of these situations is the average measurement one to be desired. Similarly with personal adjustment and the necessity of establishing criteria by which good or wholesome adjustment can be recognized and sought. Adjustment should certainly resolve existing conflict. Natural responses to frustration, such as aggression, can be directed into appropriate channels. Aggression, rather than being unleashed against persons, can be useful motivation to attack the problem itself. The first criterion of healthy adjustment, therefore, is that it be *psychologically sound* (Table 21).

Table 21.   Criteria of Healthy Adjustment*

Criterion	Advocated By	
1. Psychologically sound		
2. Socially acceptable	Contemporary psychology	Christian psychology
3. Morally sound		

*Patterned after Schneiders (1965)

A second consideration is the effect of the solution on other persons. A child frustrated in a nursery situation because of an insufficient number of playthings should not resolve frustration by taking toys from another child. Similarly, an employee not obtaining a raise should not release frustration by deliberately lowering his work standards. Adjustment, to be healthy, should not have antisocial qualities, but rather should be *socially acceptable*.

These first two requirements of good adjustment are advocated by most contemporary authorities in mental health. There is a third requisite, however, that is rarely proposed and in most instances avoided. This is the criterion that adjustment be *morally sound*. According to Christian psychology, adjustment that involves moral behavior should conform to the laws of morality, such as the Ten Commandments. Consider the case of a woman falling in love with a married man. Frustrated, the woman seeks counsel. The contemporary psychologist would likely condone pursuing the illicit affair, if it brings release of conflict for the two people involved. However, this behavior, although psychologically sound (assuming it does not produce guilt) and socially acceptable (reflected in majority behavior), violates two commandments, one forbidding adultery and the other forbidding the coveting of another's spouse. From the Christian point of view, therefore, healthy adjustment, when it involves moral issues, should meet the criterion of moral soundness.

With these three criteria of healthy adjustment in mind, the growth and development of the individual may be examined next. Personality development involves five areas—physical, intellectual, social, moral, and emotional. The first four areas will be discussed in this chapter, and emotional development reserved for the following chapter.

PHYSICAL MATURITY

Physical maturity refers here not only to chronological age but also to physical hygiene, health and dietary habits, and recreational activity. In an age in which physical achievement is so highly regarded—consider the Little League, athletic scholarships, and professional sports—the average American youngster is usually motivated to excel in athletic endeavor. But this emphasis on physiological development can induce deep inferiority feelings in handicapped children and adolescents, and in aspirants failing to qualify for team selection. Other areas of physical development giving rise to similar adjustment problems include reading, speech, and hearing difficulties, as well as problems of excessive underweight or overweight.

Prevention or cure of most physical maladjustment problems can be effected by good physical hygiene. Proper dietary habits, dental care, and regular medical checkups in early life can usually preclude later adolescent health problems. Within the school systems, recreational facilities and programs should be available to all, not just to the athlete. The handicapped individual requires help in specialized programs.

INTELLECTUAL MATURITY

Intellectual maturity is usually defined in terms of I.Q. However, the term will be used here to refer to all cognitive growth, including aptitudes (innate), abilities (acquired), achievement, formal and informal education, work experience, and motivational habits. Self-knowledge, a sense of humor, and acceptance of authority can also be considered as aspects of intellectual maturity.

Related problem areas are exemplified in the lack of vocational objectives, unrealistic levels of aspiration, poor study habits, disciplinary problems, and low motivation. Prevention or correction of intellectual maladjustment can be accomplished by adequate vocational and educational guidance, and the development of programs for exceptional children, adolescents, and adults. For adolescents, particularly, an esteem for rightful law, order, and authority should be cultivated, as well as an explanation of their necessity for a civilized society. Otherwise, the adolescent will find great difficulty in controlling a natural urge to defy the existing order of things. Rebellion against the authority of parents, school teachers, and community officials is manifested in today's younger generation.

According to the Christian viewpoint, authority originates in God and is expressed in his commandments. By virtue of public office, established for the common welfare, men partake of that authority. Their governing power, however, is attached to the office, not to their person. Man is intended by God to act lawfully and according to reason. This precept, however, does not preclude the right to resort to force of arms when inequities are imposed by unlawful government.

Authority, to be individually meaningful, must be internalized. Parents are at times shocked by the behavior of sons and daughters away from home, particularly in view of what was considered to be a righteous upbringing. A common fault of parents, however, is continual imposition of *external* authority. The child must be taught to *internalize* discipline, so that he will carry within himself, wherever he might go, self-government and self-control.

The necessity of work is vital to intellectual growth. All youngsters should be given the opportunity to work, even if they are not required to do so because of family finances. Work accomplishes more than educating a person about the value of money or the wisdom of a budget. It brings the young person into contact with those of other socioeconomic strata. It also gives an appreciation of the value and dignity of labor, whether it be simple or complex.

SOCIAL MATURITY

Social skills and the facility of getting along with people constitute social maturity. Etiquette, poise, and the art of conversation are included, as well those as qualities that rank high in "personality" contests.

Problems relating to inadequate social maturity include shyness, introversion, extraversion, feelings of economic and social inferiority, and finding one's place in the social world.

Social education should begin as early as kindergarten age. Children should be taught to share toys and to participate in group play. Etiquette classes and dancing instruction can be introduced in youthful years. In high school, adolescents should be encouraged to become involved in activities that will enhance social growth, such as dramatics, clubs, and school publications. These activities, while they must not interfere with academic work, are vital to personality development. The ability to get along with others is an asset required for progress in every field of human endeavor.

On the college campus there is a social situation which can be inadvertently a source of much insecurity and anxiety, and that is the fraternity-sorority system. Usually, wherever these groups exist they dominate the social milieu. However, since these organizations select as members but a certain percentage of students, those remaining unchosen feel keenly a social stigma. Although privately supported institutions may set discriminatory standards of social acceptability, this situation would seem an injustice in a state university. The state institution is supported by public taxes. If social groups are to be a part of the state university, there should be no discrimination in membership that would leave a minority of students socially ostracized. A solution would be to have a number of social organizations sufficient to include the possibility of total student membership. Private country clubs have their place, but not in institutions supported by public funds.

MORAL MATURITY

Moral or religious maturity can be defined as the degree to which a person is aware of his correct origin, purpose, and ultimate destiny. The questions to be answered are, Where did I come from? Why am I here? and Where am I going? The purpose of man's existence should not be settled arbitrarily by hypothetical or theoretical solutions, for sincerity is not a good criterion of objective truth. Man's capacity for attaining absolute certitude has been demonstrated, and it should be applied to this problem above all others. A later section of this book discusses this issue at length.

For purposes of the present chapter, the Judeo-Christian frame of reference is taken as the norm against which moral maturity is to be measured. Therefore, the closer one's behavior conforms to this frame of reference the greater will be his moral growth. This kind of moral maturity will be defined as *objective moral maturity*. However, there are many people who are invincibly ignorant of the Judeo-Christian moral code, and yet who are following the dictates of conscientious convictions—for instance, those who have never heard of the Ten Commandments or of Christ. Such individuals can be described as possessing *subjective moral maturity*. They may also be more pleasing to God than those possessing the truth but not following it. A conscientious atheist would have greater subjective moral maturity than a lax Christian. Obviously, God is the only intelligence capable of making any valid comparative judgments among men. (For further treatment of subjective and objective morality, see Chapter 13.)

Moral and religious maturity is not definable only as one's relationship with God. It also embraces relationships with one's fellow man, both within the family and within the community. The person professing to pray much and to be a good Christian, and yet not concerning himself with the welfare of the poor, the socially and the economically oppressed, is deluding himself. Love of neighbor is a commandment second only to that of love of God. And who is one's neighbor? Not just the person next door or down the street, and not just the people in one's community. All the people in the world are one's neighbor.

Lastly, moral and religious maturity can be applied on a higher social level, that of nations. A society's orientation to God is indicative of its moral maturity. A theistically oriented society, such as the Judeo-Christian or Islamic, therefore has greater objective moral maturity than one atheistically oriented.

Problems relating to moral and religious maturity can be grouped in accordance with the social levels already discussed. Internationally, there is the problem of war. Nuclear conflict and ultimate self-destruction will be avoidable only when nations begin to implement policies based on moral precepts, of which the Judeo-Christian code is the highest example. Only when nations treat one another as they desire to be treated will war finally be abolished. Where there is love, there can be no hate, and where there is no hate, there can be no war.

Moral problems *within* nations and communities center on socioeconomic oppression. An understanding of basic human liberties, including the right to a just living wage, as well as the obligation to eliminate poverty and to take care of the sick and the aged, illuminates problems that national and local government can and should resolve. Poverty is defined here as the deprivation of those goods, material and intellectual, to which all men are entitled (Abbott, 1966).

On the family level, there are the moral problems dealing with the husband-wife relationship and the parent-child relationship. Marriage itself involves moral aspects of sex and of fidelity.

On the individual level, everyone is faced with the duty to seek moral and religious truth, to educate his moral perspective, and to carry out obligations thereby realized. To do less is unworthy of the dignity of man and the heights to which he can aspire (Abbott, 1966).

The ultimate problem facing the individual is the threat of nonexistence, or death. Since this reality is discussed in a later section of this book, it will only be mentioned here as a problem relevant to moral and religious maturity.

How can moral and religious maturity be developed? In the present age of communications there is no longer a valid excuse for moral ignorance. Knowledge is available; it is the obligation of the individual to seek it. Personal study and prayer are the first steps in developing moral maturity. One should guard against the common rationalization of retaining ignorance in the hope that such ignorance will excuse immoral behavior.

The educational field can also be of assistance to moral development. The school systems, from grade school through college, could schedule released-time classes during the week for moral and religious instruction. Credit could be and should be given for such courses. Nor should this provision be construed as a violation of the separation of church and state. The state can benefit by the moral training of future citizens. Millions of dollars are lost in crime, and many more are expended in the apprehension and containment of the offender. If for no other reason, it would be economically expedient for the state to take an active interest in the moral education of youth. The greater the degree to which the state ignores the moral training of its members, the greater will be the degree of immoral behavior and crime. The policy of the separation of church and state, originally intended to prevent the establishment of a state religion, has in modern times become exaggerated to a ridiculous political extreme.

Chapter 11

Healthy Emotional Adjustment

Emotional stability, freedom from anxiety, self-control, a sense of humor —all of these factors constitute emotional maturity. Internalization of authority, discussed under intellectual maturity, is also relevant.

Problems relating to lack of emotional maturity may be summarized in the term *emotional disorganization*, which includes excessive repression, depression, daydreaming, continual conflict, and neurotic patterns of behavior. Such emotional reactions are usually consequent to frustration (Figure 13).

Prevention, or cure, of emotional maladjustment can be effected in many ways. The suggestions to follow may also be applicable to other areas of personality growth, since it is the whole person that is being considered. Healthy emotional adjustment in childhood, adolescence, and adulthood will be sequentially treated.

EMOTIONAL ADJUSTMENT IN THE CHILD

A number of conditions are essential for the child's healthy emotional development (Table 22).

1. A first requisite is *peace in the home*. The child is greatly affected by any

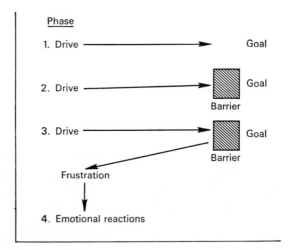

FIG. 13.   Sequential phases in the production of frustration and emotional reactivity.

Table 22.   Requisites for Emotional Adjustment in the Child

1.   Peace in the home
2.   Love, affection, and understanding
3.   Participation in family objectives
4.   Discipline
5.   Independence
6.   Social life with peers
7.   Achievement
8.   Emotional expression
9.   Moral training

display of hostility between those he loves, particularly his parents. A minor argument between parents can appear, in a child's perception, to be a real battle. Parental disagreements in the presence of children should be conducted unemotionally.

2. *Love, affection, and understanding* are essential to childhood security. They should be bestowed in large doses to every child, independent of the degree to which the child responds. Parents should not make the mistake of giving affection only to those children who react appreciatively. On the other hand, overprotection, whether as excessive indulgence or excessive dominance, should be avoided (Schneiders, 1965).

3. *Participation in family objectives* can begin in early childhood. Sharing in future plans gives the child a sense of belonging, as well as of responsibility.

4. *Discipline* is deeply needed. Children not receiving deserved parental correction may, through their need for guilt removal, behave even worse in order to solicit punishment. External discipline in childhood is a step prior to internalization of authority in adolescence.

5. *Independence*, in the sense of the child's perceiving himself as an individual, should be encouraged. Each child has a unique personality and a corresponding place in the family setting.

6. *Social life* with other children aids development of emotional maturity. The importance of social interaction has already been discussed under social maturity.

7. The *need for achievement* should be met. Even casual observation will identify early aptitudes and talents, and opportunities for their development should be structured.

8. *Emotional expression*, particularly that of frustration and anger, should be permitted, although the child should be taught healthy direction for such catharsis. When punished, he naturally has temporary feelings of frustration and hostility. The direction of anger should not be one of open defiance of authority, such as impertinence. However, slamming a door, stamping a foot, or muttering under the breath may well serve as acceptable releases of emotional tension.

9. *Moral training*, vitally essential to healthy emotional adjustment, should begin in childhood. Conscience is basically an innate function of intelligence and, as such, is inborn. (See Chapter 13.) This moral awareness, however, must be educated in matters of moral rightness and wrongness. Childhood is the beginning. Before the child is two years of age he should have learned that parents are to be obeyed and that disobedience is punishable. Guilt requires cleansing and reparation. The child permitted to go unpunished for acts he realizes to be wrong will never develop healthy emotional stability. Unerased guilt sets the stage for anxiety and neurosis.

EMOTIONAL ADJUSTMENT IN THE ADOLESCENT

The teenager's biggest problem is finding his place in contemporary society. The transition from childhood to adulthood can be most painful. Therefore, the adolescent requires patient understanding, combined, how-

ever, with a firm hand. In addition to those needs relating to childhood, a
number of others can be added (Table 23).

Table 23.   Requisites for Emotional Adjustment in the Adolescent

1. Internalization of authority
2. Spiritual or religious frame of reference
3. Acceptance of responsibility
4. Varied activity
5. Development of emotional adequacy and depth

1. *Internalization of authority*, mentioned in the treatment of intellectual
maturity, also contributes strongly to proper emotional development. The
adolescent storm lies more within than without. The teenager must internalize norms of conduct that will control emotion and passion in their early
growth. He should acquire an appreciation for, and practice of, self-control
and self-discipline. Lack of these character traits not only induces emotional
maladjustment but can lead to later neurosis.

2. The development of *a spiritual* or *religious frame of reference* is essential to the adolescent's striving for stability. The general moral principles
given in childhood need greater depth and comprehensiveness to be of
practical value to the teenager. Opportunity should be provided for religious instruction, and youth should be taught how spiritual growth fosters
emotional maturity. Particularly in the area of sexual behavior the adolescent needs moral guidance. Sexuality divorced from morality is but animal
behavior. (See Chapter 13.)

3. *Acceptance of responsibility* induces self-confidence and self-reliance,
both necessary for emotional stability. Acceptance of responsibility also
teaches one to face reality, rather than to flee its problems. The habit of
shouldering obligations can be inculcated in childhood, although it is even
more essential in teenage years. The person unaccustomed to carrying out
responsible tasks will tend, as the years pass, to avoid obligations increasingly, to the point of neurotic withdrawal from social contact.

4. *Varied activity* is helpful in determining where skills and talents lie.
The teenage years should be used to probe strengths and weaknesses, in
terms of endeavor in various interest areas, whether in or out of school.
Subsequent success and failure will bring knowledge of personal capabilities and limitations, as well as point the way toward realistic life goals.

5. *Development of emotional adequacy and depth* is a need not always
recognized by the adolescent, but nonetheless deserving of his attention.
The ability to empathize with those less fortunate in life or with those whom
tragedy has struck brings insight into true values. Teenagers should be en-

couraged to visit the sick and to become involved in community projects aiding the unfortunate. A fundamental characteristic of the neurotic is self-concern. The cultivation of concern for others is a strong bulwark against such egocentricity, and also helps a person to be satisfied with his own condition in life.

EMOTIONAL ADJUSTMENT IN THE ADULT

In addition to the considerations discussed in the emotional development of the child and the adolescent, other contributing factors can be cultivated on the adult level (Table 24). Indeed, emotional growth is a lifelong process, and one that requires continual shaping.

1. *Multiple interests* become especially important in later years. Without them, the transition from the active life to a quiet routine of retirement can become a source of restlessness and discontent. Hobbies and unstrenuous

Table 24. Aids to Emotional Adjustment in the Adult

1. Multiple interests
2. Sense of humor
3. Ability to relax
4. Setting a time for decisions
5. Living in the present
6. Avoiding hate, anger, jealousy, envy, bitterness, and depression
7. Controlling release of hostility
8. Reinterpreting situations
9. Accepting reality
10. Accepting imperfections in oneself and in others
11. Insight, self-understanding
12. Realistic level of aspiration
13. Well-defined goals
14. Integration of ideals with conduct
15. Building a frustration-tolerance threshold
16. Recognizing frustration-aggression
17. Recognizing free-floating anxiety
18. Recognizing repression
19. Learning when to seek help
20. Practicing unselfishness
21. Learning to forgive
22. Being flexible in having one's own way
23. A correct philosophy of suffering
24. Learning to love

athletic skills should be developed in life's middle years, to afford quiet enjoyment and relaxed use of time later. The elderly citizen often feels useless
and a social encumbrance. A busy life helps to preclude social withdrawal
and eventual self-pity.

2. A *sense of humor*, the ability to laugh at life and not to take oneself
too seriously, is a good asset to emotional adjustment. Humor, of course,
can also be "sick," in the improper attachment of levity to a person, place,
or thing. The so-called cruelty joke is an example, as are jokes of obvious
vulgarity, crudity, or sacrilege. The person who enjoys perverted humor is
himself sick, in that he seeks to destroy what is deserving of respect. A come-
dian who uses vulgarity or obscenity does so to derive pleasure from the
shocked response he elicits from the audience or to release verbally his own
frustration caused by a jaded and meaningless personal life. Too, such a
performer often has a paradoxical contempt for the applause he receives.
The same motives are attributable to the school teacher or the college
professor who uses vulgar or obscene lecture material. For healthy emotional development, therefore, a proper sense of humor should be cultivated.
The insight of humor comes more easily to some people, but is nonetheless
within the grasp of everyone.

3. In this hectic whirl of contemporary living, the *ability to relax*, to slow
down, is essential to mental quietude. The day should be planned so that
for at least half an hour one can withdraw for a period of mental contem-
plation and relaxation. How time scurries past—and how often one is
caught up in activity that seems like a treadmill. A daily quiet break affords
the opportunity for reevaluation of planned engagements and pursuits.

4. Related to relaxation is the wisdom of *setting a time for making decisions*. The hour of day one feels best is the time to resolve personal problems and to make personal commitments. Usually the morning is preferable, for the evening is fraught with the accumulated mental and physical fatigue of the day. Of course, there are always emergency situations
requiring immediate attention, but these are the exception, not the rule.

5. Many people are continually unhappy because they dwell on ills and
misfortune that may or may not lie ahead. One should practice, therefore,
living in the present. From the Christian point of view, it is not wise, or
possible, to carry tomorrow's cross with today's grace (Boylan, 1954).
Sufficient are the problems of today, and sufficient the grace to endure
them. God in his wisdom will give strength to meet the need. To worry
about what could happen in the future is a needless worry. Experience
proves that many things worried about never happen, and the things we

should be concerned about, and are not, do. Although it is good to plan for the future and to take reasonable precautions, it is emotionally unhealthful, and unnecessary, to indulge in anxiety about future contingencies.

6. Not only should needless anxiety be avoided. Other unhealthy emotional responses should be resisted. This means *avoiding hate, anger, jealousy, envy, bitterness, and depression.* The first two emotions involve heightened sympathetic neural reaction, which, if continued, can be physiologically damaging. Hate and anger are cancerous emotions. Left uncontrolled, they become obsessive, destroying all peace of mind. Jealousy, the fear of losing what one has, and envy, the desire for what one does not possess, are emotionally unhealthy reactions to problematic situations that will always be encountered in life. Persons who are unduly ambitious will suffer more in these instances than will those who are content with their lot in life. Bitterness and depression are reactions often consequent to personal failure, the first occurring when others are blamed, and the second when oneself is blamed or when things seem quite hopeless. For the Christian, however, indulgence in such moods indicates a lack of trust in divine providence. All things, even failure, can be offered as prayer or as penance, with the expression of trust that God will eventually lift the mantle of darkness and the weight of the cross. (See Chapter 14.) If depression or bitterness still remains after spiritual resignation, the next best course of action is diversion. Keeping constructively busy will hasten the passing of any mood.

7. Related to avoiding anger is *controlling release of hostility.* Here again constructive activity is important. Anger is analogous to boiling steam; it must be released. To suppress it completely may result in what has been termed internal aggression, exemplified by the peptic ulcer. The better way is overt expression, but in a healthy manner. For example, physical recreation is a good safety valve. It is difficult to be angry after swimming fifty yards, running a mile, or doing thirty push-ups. Hard work is another healthy release, whether in the form of attacking a text assignment, painting the fence, cleaning up the basement, or washing the car. In time the anger will pass, and one will later be thankful that the aggression was not directed toward a human target. The saying "Speak in haste, and repent at leisure" has much significance for emotional health.

8. In the busy world of human contact, the mistake can be made of assuming that one's interpretation of another person's behavior is always right and never wrong. Defensiveness can become an unhealthy emotional attitude. Therefore, the necessity for *reinterpreting situations* is essential for a wholesome, balanced perspective of others' motives. A common example

is that of being jostled in a crowd. The usual immediate reaction is one of personal resentment, as if the shove were intentional. Later reflection usually indicates the incident to have been accidental. And how often is the lack of a reply to one's greeting a passerby taken as a personal insult. The possibility of the other person's being deep in thought and consequently unaware of the greeting is not usually considered. To preserve emotional tranquility, it is necessary to reinterpret the actions of others, to give them the benefit of the doubt.

9. *Accepting reality*, instead of wishful thinking, is necessary to healthy emotional development. Repression, the unconscious but purposive tendency to push unpleasant facts below the level of awareness, can lead to avoidance of problems that should be faced and resolved. Repressed facts are not banished for long; they sooner or later return, most likely inducing anxiety.

10. Related to acceptance of reality is the *acceptance of imperfections in oneself and in others*. Irritating habits of acquaintances should not be allowed to disturb one's own serenity. It is very likely that one's own habits bother other people (who may be more charitable in this regard than oneself). Concerning personal faults, there is that noteworthy prayer requesting the wisdom to discern what can and cannot be changed. What is subject to improvement should, of course, be corrected. Faults or imperfections not amenable to correction, e.g., intellectual and physical limitations or handicaps, should be accepted. To worry about them or to continue to attempt correction will lead only to frustration and depression.

11. In consequence, *insight or self-understanding* is vital to emotional stability. The ancient Greek maxim "Know thyself" is applicable to every generation. Self-knowledge, however, is quite difficult. The mechanism of repression blocks awareness of the negative aspects of one's personality. If successful, self-analysis has another danger—the discovery of undesirable traits for which there is no apparent corrective solution. Therefore, the help and advice of those trained in personality evaluation should be sought. Once attained, self-knowledge brings a clearer perception of goals and interpersonal relationships, as well as an appreciation of the virtue of humility.

12. Associated with self-knowledge is the need for a *realistic level of aspiration*. Psychologists speak of overachievers and underachievers, the former having excess drive and the latter failing in motivation. A third category might be termed the "misachiever," the person who expects to attain goals far byond personal capability. The author recalls a student who had adopted a schedule of work and schooling which permitted but

four hours of sleep nightly. The unreasonable assumption of such capability eventually led to a neurotic breakdown.

13. *Well-defined goals* and a ranking of their importance greatly assist career planning, as well as affording the security of a planned future. Frequent conflict between temporally opposed goals, e.g., studying or going to a movie, is often the result of confused goal-orientation. There are times when the relaxation of a movie should take precedence over continual study effort. Recognition of the relative importance of goals at various times depends on a clear picture of the overall end toward which life is directed.

14. A subtle defense mechanism that can produce anxiety and emotional maladjustment is logic-tight compartmentalization, the unconscious division of conflicting areas of cognition. For example, a businessman may consider himself a good Christian, yet manipulate people as rungs up his ladder of success. The office worker may claim the virtue of honesty, yet use office stationery for private correspondence. Or again, the company car may be used for personal rather than company business. In these situations, any accusation of theft would evoke indignant denial. Racial discrimination by self-professed Christians is a further example of logic-tight compartmentalization, for there is the failure to see the contradiction between discrimination and the basic Christian precept to love one's neighbor as oneself is loved. Therefore, the *integration of ideals with conduct* is essential to healthy personality development. Recognition of inconsistencies that may exist among behavioral patterns is a necessity for mental peace.

15. As disappointments and failures in life are encountered, a new task arises: *building a frustration-tolerance threshold*, the capability of enduring psychological stress. This threshold can be compared analogously to a dike. The height of a dike determines the point of overflow, and consequently a high dike (high frustration-tolerance threshold) can withstand rising waters (frustration) better than a low dike (low frustration-tolerance threshold). It should be obvious that high frustration-tolerance is desirable for emotional maturity. Fortunately, it is within everyone's grasp. Frustration-tolerance can be developed by the practice of self-denial, that is, self-frustration. Many exert self-denial for material gain, by saving money for a new car or by forgoing desserts to lose weight. But how many are willing to practice self-denial for the greater psychological value of acquiring personal happiness in a frustrating world? Here again an analogy is helpful. Often a fire-fighter will build a fire to stop a fire. That is, the forest ranger will purposely burn out a strip of land in advance of a forest inferno. Upon

reaching this prepared area, the fire will stop, since there is no timber to aid further progress. Similarly, the practice of self-denial, or self-frustration, will prepare one to adjust to future environmental frustrations whenever they occur, as well as to minimize concomitant discontent or unhappiness. The practice of self-denial has additional value for other areas of personality growth. All great religions have universally encouraged self-denial as a means of resisting future moral temptation. After one has learned to curb legitimate desires, it becomes easier to reject morally forbidden ones.

16. Another aid to development of emotional maturity is *recognizing frustration-aggression*. The frustration-aggression hypothesis states that in most instances the reaction of aggression is due to frustration (Miller et al., 1941). Whenever one feels aggressive, whether in thought, word, or deed, it is well to pause a moment and introspectively examine one's feelings for hidden frustration. Particularly in times of tension and stress does aggressive behavior manifest itself, lashing out at persons or objects. Mindful of these facts, one can search out hidden sources of frustration, thereby removing the undesirable emotional consequence of aggression.

17. *Recognizing free-floating anxiety* is another aid to emotional adjustment. When this reaction (discussed in Chapter 8) is detected, one should attempt to determine and remove the causal factors.

18. At the root of free-floating anxiety and other defense mechanisms, notably that of rationalization, is repression and *recognizing repression* is another essential aid. Intended as nature's defense against psychological threat, repression can nevertheless reach such proportions as to prevent realistic self-knowledge. When other people offer criticisms that one feels are unjust and undeserved, one would do well to look for the personal error of repression.

19. If personal attempts to resolve conflict have failed, one should, when it is appropriate, *learn to seek help*. Pride can be a stumbling block here. Even though one may be capable of advising another in an identical situation, it is more difficult when the circumstances are personal, for then an objective viewpoint is highly difficult.

20. A great help to emotional development is *the practice of unselfishness*. Egocentricity is the core of neurosis. Self-centeredness should therefore be avoided and fought against. Self-pity, another expression of ego-concern, is also detrimental to healthy personality development. Unselfishness should be continuously cultivated throughout life. The scriptural statement that he who loves life will lose it and he who denies himself will find life has much psychological value (Matt. 16:24–26). The happiest people in the

world are those who forget self and spend their lives in the service of others.

21. It has been seen that the emotional reaction of hatred is detrimental to emotional stability. An excellent means of avoiding this behavioral response is *learning to forgive*. Frequently, the person who hates has assumed that self-preservation and status must be preserved at all costs. But sufficient reflection on one's own imperfections and faults should help understand weakness in others. When one is offended, therefore, the benefit of any doubt regarding the offender's intention should be granted. If it is ascertained that another person has *deliberately* offended, then one should endeavor to determine why. The author, a Catholic, has been offended at times by atheistic colleagues. However, closer examination of the situation has indicated that the offender has become subject to certain negative emotional biases concerning Catholicism. Or, unfortunately, the biased person has encountered unworthy Catholics who have set a bad example or who have in ignorance communicated a false interpretation of Catholic teaching. Of course, there are always the few who enjoy being offensive, but such persons eventually alienate themselves from others as well, and therefore should not be allowed to disturb one's own peace of mind.

22. *Flexibility in one's personal will* is helpful to emotional tranquility. With regard to moral absolutes, deviation is obviously erroneous. But there are many areas of human interaction in which one's own preference can give way. There is rarely but one way an objective can be accomplished, and there should be no compulsion to enforce one's own choice or decision in such instances. Whether it be in business, community affairs, social activities, or family matters, one should keep a mind open to others' opinions. The decision to follow another's rather than one's own preference should even be deliberately exercised, as practice against the habit of assuming personal opinion to be the best.

23. *A correct philosophy of suffering* is essential for maximal peace of mind. The person who has not found the solution to pain, suffering, evil, and death is prey to an anxiety that pervades the deepest part of human nature. The paradox of evil is given separate treatment elsewhere, and will not be developed here. (See Chapter 14.)

24. Lastly, to attain the greatest heights of emotional development, one must *learn to love*. Love should be distinguished from infatuation and sexual attraction. Infatuation is based on the projection of desirable traits into another person, who may or may not possess them. "Love at first sight" is the example here. True love follows upon knowledge of characteristics a person actually has, whether such traits are positive or negative. True love

desires the welfare of the loved one, even to the point of self-sacrifice. Indeed, self-sacrifice is the ultimate expression of love, tendered as proof of love. The happiest people in the world are those who are in love. However, love will die if not nourished. One should strive to protect and sustain love in every human situation, whether it be marriage, family, or concern for neighbor and the less fortunate of the world. Love should express itself in charitable work, for love without a giving of oneself is arid and meaningless. (See Chapter 16.)

THE TOTAL MAN

It should be noted that a person progresses differentially in the five areas of physical, intellectual, social, moral, and emotional growth. Therefore, it is possible for an intellectual genius to be a moral idiot. This fact should be recalled when one hears, for example, of an eminent scientist questioning the validity of a moral principle. The halo of knowledge in a specified field of knowledge should not be extended to areas in which a person is incompetent or unqualified.

In conclusion, it would be well to strive for continued self-evaluation in these five areas of growth, as did Ben Franklin, who kept a notebook on his progress toward attainment of desirable personality traits. The fruit of many such years of motivated self-improvement will be strength of character, stability of emotion, wisdom of thought, and peace of mind in a world of frustration, conflict, and turmoil.

PART III   SUGGESTED READINGS

Allport, G. *The person in psychology*. Boston: Beacon, 1968. Part II. "Personal Conditions for Growth."
Allport, G. W. *Pattern and growth in personality*. New York: Holt, Rinehart, and Winston, 1961. Ch. 12. "The Mature Personality."
Arnold, M., and Gasson, J. *The human person*. New York: Ronald, 1954. Ch. 13. "Psychology as a Normative Science" (Schneiders); Ch. 16. "Logotherapy and Existential Analysis" (Arnold, Gasson).

Barron, F. *Creative person and creative process.* New York: Holt, Rinehart and Winston (paperback). Introduction; Ch. 1. "The Nature of the Problem of Creativity for the Psychologist."

Bube, R. (Ed.) *The encounter between Christianity and science.* Grand Rapids: W. B. Eerdman, 1968. Ch. 6. "Geology" (Eckelmann); Ch. 7. "Physical Science" (Bube).

Bugental, J. F. T. *Challenges of humanistic psychology.* McGraw-Hill, 1967. Ch. 7. "The Proactive Personality" (Bonner); Ch. 28. "The Process of the Basic Encounter Group" (Rogers).

Buhler, C., and Massarik, F. (Eds.) *Humanism and the course of life: Studies in goal-determination.* New York: Springer, 1968. Ch. 21. "Meaning as an Integrative Factor" (Weisskopf-Joelson).

Cavanagh, J. R., and McGoldrick, J. B. *Fundamental psychiatry* (Rev. Ed.). Milwaukee: Bruce, 1966. Ch. II. "Positive Mental Health."

Coleman, J. C. *Psychology and effective behavior.* Chicago: Scott Foresman, 1969. Part Four. "Toward Effective Adjustment and Personal Growth."

Evely. L. *Joy.* New York: Herder, 1968. Introduction: "Joy."

Frankl, V. E. *Psychotherapy and existentialism.* New York: Washington Square Press, 1967. Ch. I. "The Philiosophical Foundations of Logotherapy"; Ch. III. "Beyond Self-Actualization and Self-Expression."

Frankl, V. E. *The doctor and the soul.* New York: Alfred A. Knopf, 1966. Introduction; Part IIA. "General Existential Analyses"; Part IV. "From Secular Confession to Medical Ministry."

Frankl, V. E. *Man's search for meaning.* New York: Washington Square Press, 1963. Part Two: "Basic Concepts of Logotherapy."

Fromm, E. *Escape from freedom.* New York: Holt, Rinehart and Winston, 1941. (Also Avon Books, 1966.) Ch. II. "The Emergence of the Individual and the Ambiguity of Freedom"; Ch. V. "Mechanisms of Escape."

Fromm, E. *The art of loving.* New York: Harper & Row (paperback), 1956. Part II, 3: "The Objects of Love."

Fromm, E. *The sane society.* New York: Holt, Rinehart and Winston, 1955. Ch. 3. "The Human Situation—The Key to Humanistic Psychoanalysis."

Horney, K. *Our inner conflicts.* New York: Norton, 1945. Part I. "Neurotic Conflicts and Attempts at Solutions."

Jourard, S. M. *The transparent self: Self-disclosure and well-being.* Princeton: D. von Nostrand (paperback), 1954. Ch. 2. "Self-Disclosure: The Scientist's Portal to a Man's Soul."

Kemp, C. G. *Intangibles in counseling.* New York: Houghton Mifflin, 1967. Ch. 6. "Modern Values"; Ch. 7. "Anxiety;" Ch. 8. "Freedom and Responsibility"; Ch. 9. "Search for Meaning."

Keniston, K. *The uncommitted.* New York: Dell (Delta paperback), 1965. Ch. 7. "Major Themes of Alienation"; Ch. 8. "Chronic Change and the Cult of the Present"; Ch. 9. "The Division of Life"; Ch. 11. "The Decline of Utopia."

Maslow, A. H. *Toward a psychology of being*. Princeton: van Nostrand (paperback), 1962. Ch. 3. "Deficiency Motivation and Growth Motivation"; Ch. 6. "Cognition of Being in Peak-Experiences"; Ch. 11. "Psychological Data and Human Values"; Ch. 12. "Values, Growth, and Health."

May, R. *Psychology and the human dilemma*. Princeton: van Nostrand, 1967. Part Two. "Sources of Anxiety."

May, R. *Man's search for himself*. New York: Norton, 1953. Ch. 1. "The Loneliness and Anxiety of Modern Man"; Ch. 2. "The Roots of Our Malady."

May, R. *The meaning of anxiety*. New York: Ronald, 1950. Ch. 4. "Anxiety Interpreted Psychologically"; Ch. 5. "Anxiety Interpreted Culturally."

Moore, T. V. *The driving forces of human nature and their adjustment*. New York: Grune & Stratton, 1948. Ch. 19. "Desire."

Mowrer, O. H. *Morality and mental health*. Chicago: Rand McNally, 1967. Ch. 6. "The New Pornography" (*Time* Magazine); Ch. 18. "Reality Therapy—A New Approach" (Glasser); Ch. 61. "A Historical Explanation of Alienation" (Stroup); Ch. 70. "Decadence and Irresponsibility" (Whittier).

Mowrer, O. H. *The crisis in psychiatry and religion*. Princeton: Van Nostrand, 1961. Ch. 1. "Some Philosophical Problems in Psychological Counseling."

Rogers, C. R. *On becoming a person*. Boston: Houghton-Mifflin, 1961. Ch. 1. "This Is Me."

Royce, J. R. *The encapsulated man: An interdisciplinary essay on the search for meaning*. Princeton: Van Nostrand, 1964. Ch. 7. "Meaning, Value, and Personality."

Schneiders, A. A. *Personality dynamics and mental health* (Rev. Ed.). New York: Holt, Rinehart and Winston, 1965. Ch. 2. "Some Basic Concepts and Criteria of Adjustment and Mental Health"; Ch. 15. "Religion and Mental Hygiene."

Severin, F. T. *Humanistic viewpoints in psychology*. New York: McGraw-Hill, 1965. Ch. 36. "Value Orientation in Counseling" (Williamson); Ch. 37. "Psychology, Religion, and Values for the Counselor" (Wrenn).

Sheen, F. J. *Peace of soul*. Garden City, N.Y.: Doubleday (Image paperback), 1964. Ch. 1. "Frustration"; Ch. 2. "The Philosophy of Anxiety"; Ch. 5. "Morbidity and the Denial of Guilt"; Ch. 8. "Sex and the Love of God."

Sheen, F. J. *Lift up your heart*. Garden City, N.Y.: Doubleday (Image paperback), 1955. Ch. 5. "The Philosophy of Pleasure"; Ch. 14. "Man's Capacity for Self Transcendence"; Ch. 17. "Beyond the Merely Human."

Sutich, A., and Vich, M. (Eds.) *Readings in humanistic psychology*. New York: Free Press, 1969. Ch. 2. "Notes on Being-Psychology" (Maslow); Ch. 4. "Human Life Goals in the Humanistic Perspective" (Buhler); Ch. 5. "Self-Transcendence as a Human Phenomenon" (Frankl); Ch. 11. "The Necessary and Sufficient Conditions of Creativity" (Hallman).

Tillich, P. *The courage to be*. New Haven: Yale University Press, 1952. Ch. 2. "Being, Non-Being, and Anxiety."

PART IV

HUMAN DESTINY

Thus far this book has dealt with man's basic nature and general growth. There remains the analysis of the core of human nature, the human spirit, together with its yearning for ultimate meaning and survival. Chapter 12 looks at the fundamental question of the existence of God. The relationship of God to man, in terms of human moral behavior, is discussed in Chapter 13. Chapter 14 touches on the paradox of evil and suffering in human experience, with the Christian response. Chapter 15 explores the crux of all Christian theory, namely, the personality of Christ. In conclusion Chapter 16 presents the intimate relationship between God and man, and its significance for the individual.

Chapter 12

The Reality of God

For the Christian psychologist, God is the Alpha and the Omega (Rev. 1:8) and is the center of psychological theory. Without God, a Christian psychology would be meaningless, an imaginative fantasy.

The demonstration of the existence of God and the communication of this fact to others constitute two separate problems. Man, possessing dual capabilities of knowing and assenting, can recognize the path of logic and yet still reject inescapable conclusions. A paradoxical aspect of human freedom is the ability to deny what is intellectually realized to be true. In this chapter, the problem of God's existence will be discussed first, followed by a critique of the reasons his existence is not conceded by atheistic psychologies.

THE EXISTENCE OF GOD

The capability of the human mind to attain absolute certitude has been illustrated by analysis (in Chapter 3) of the Principle of Contradiction. This principle is the basis on which God's existence can be demonstrated. The starting point is the acknowledgment of causal sequence in the world. Causality is considered here not to be a theoretical abstraction, but rather an empirical experience. Some psychologists, as noted in previous chapters,

137

deny the ontological reality of causality, and have substituted correlation. However, it seems that evidence, e.g., the simple illustration of a kick in the posterior anatomy, can be deduced for the validity of cause-and-effect relationships. In such an instance, the rejection of causality and a discussion on correlational relationships appear quite absurd. The denial of ontological causality is, of course, a Kantian heritage, and those who follow Kant in this regard must solve their own problems of reconciling empirical experience with a speculative metaphysics.

For present purposes, therefore, the objective reality of cause-and-effect relationships is the starting point of the proof of God's existence. The sequential chain of causes and effects leads naturally to the questions of how it all started and whether or not there was a beginning, or first cause. The term *first cause* is synonymous with God, since God is essentially the Existence prior to whom there is no existence, i.e., God was not brought into existence by something else. Therefore, the question, Was there a first cause? is identical with the question, Does God exist?

The only two possible answers to this query are, There was a first cause, and There was not a first cause. The reason that these are the only two possibilities is that they are mutually exclusive. Now, there are two procedures by which the initial question can be answered. One alternative can be shown to be true, or the other alternative can be shown to be false. The first way could be considered a *direct* approach, and the second way an *indirect* approach. It should be noted that the indirect approach is a valid procedure only with two alternatives that are mutually exclusive. Thus, if it can be shown that the nonexistence of a first cause is a false premise, then the only possible alternative, namely, the existence of a first cause, must be true. Instead, therefore, of a *direct* proof for the existence of a first cause, an *indirect* approach will be followed, in the demonstration that the alternative, "nonexistence of a first cause," is false.

Let it be assumed for the moment that the nonexistence of a first cause is the true alternative. Now, if this were true, then there would have been no second cause, or third cause, or ultimately, in the sequential chain of causes, no presently existing causes. This final conclusion, the negation of presently existing causality, contradicts empirical experience. The premise from which a false conclusion is logically drawn must itself be false; therefore, the premise "nonexistence of a first cause" is false. It then follows that the only alternative possible, existence of a first cause, must be true. In summary, the existence of a first cause, or God, has been proven by demonstrating the only possible alternative to be absurd.

It should be noted once more that this procedure is valid only in the instance of two mutually exclusive alternatives. Thus, for example, a color cannot be proved to be yellow by proving it is not orange. To prove a color to be yellow, it would have to be shown that it is *not* "non-yellow," which includes all colors other than yellow.

THE UNCAUSED CAUSE

The question may arise at this point, What caused the first cause? This question is based on a misunderstanding of the Principle of Causality, which states that all *effects* must have causes, but which does not assert that all *causes* must have causes. The confusion arises because in most instances an experience of a cause is that it is the effect of some preceding cause, e.g., parents are the cause of one's existence, but parents in turn were effects of their parents. Once it is realized, however, that the Principle of Causality does not require all causes to be effects and consequently caused, it is possible to see that the first cause does not require a preceding cause. Indeed, it is its own reason for existence. Being the first cause, it precedes all other existence. For this reason, the first cause is sometimes referred to as *necessary being*. All other beings need not exist, but the first cause by necessity exists.

ETERNAL EXISTENCE

Several corollaries can be drawn from the foregoing analysis. It should be obvious that God, as first cause, is responsible for all other existences, whether as causes or effects, that have come into being. It should also be obvious that God, as necessary being, always existed. He was not brought into existence by a prior being. And if God *has* always existed, it follows that he *will* always exist, i.e., he is independent of time, eternal. For, as he is necessary being, there is no other being that can destroy him. Neither can he destroy himself, for this involves a meaningless contradiction. In conclusion, the rallying cry "God is dead" is absurd. God is not dead, although false interpretations of him may well be. Man has a tendency to form God into man's own image, but he should avoid this error and come to know God as He wishes to be known.

THE TRINITY

The Christian belief in the Trinity, i.e., three Persons in one divine nature, is based on divine revelation (G. D. Smith, 1961). The Trinity is an incomprehensible mystery, revealed to man and beyond the reach of human understanding. However, the attempt by St. Thomas Aquinas to describe the Trinity is an interesting one, and therefore is presented here (Pegis, 1944).

St. Thomas notes that if man has been made in God's image (Gen. 1:27), then careful introspection might tell man something about God's nature. Man, for example, can reflect on himself, and therefore form a self-concept, or idea of himself. God the Father, St. Thomas continues, being an intelligent being, can also reflect upon himself. Man, however, can have but an imperfect self-image. God, on the other hand, being perfect, can have a perfect self-image. In fact, God's self-reflection is so perfect that it constitutes a second Person in the divine nature. This second Person is the "Word" referred to in St. John's Gospel, "In the beginning was the Word, and the Word was with God, and the Word was God" (John 1:1). The Divine Word in St. John's Gospel is therefore this very self-reflection, or idea, that God has of himself, who is also called God the Son. The relationship between God the Father and God the Son is theologically described as a "begetting." The second Person in the Trinity is described as being begotten of the Father, and as being the only-begotten Son.

Not only does man have a self-image, but he also holds this self-concept in high regard. Man loves himself. (Indeed, one often has a higher esteem for one's own worth than does anyone else!) The reason for this is that man is naturally attracted to what is perceived as good.

On the divine level, St. Thomas observes, God also is attracted to goodness. Now, God the Father perceives in God the Son (his self-concept) perfect goodness, and God the Son (begotten as a distinct person) perceives the goodness in God the Father. Therefore, the two Persons in their mutual love, and loving each other *perfectly*, yield the third Person of the Trinity, referred to as God the Holy Spirit. Notice that God the Father and God the Son do not individually, but rather together, account for the Holy Spirit. That is why, theologically speaking, the Holy Spirit is said to have "proceeded" from God the Father *and* God the Son.

This "procession" or "spiration" of the Holy Spirit, as well as the "begetting" of the Son, is a divine mystery. Therefore, St. Thomas merely attempts to describe, in an analogy of human nature and divine nature, the relations existing within the Trinity. Neither St. Thomas nor anyone else contends that the Trinity can be understood. Indeed, the precise reason it is a revealed doctrine is because man could never have attained this truth by his rational powers alone.

DENIAL OF GOD

The "God is dead" movement has already been mentioned as an invalid denial of God's existence (Altizer, 1967). It is actually an expression of dissatisfaction with several contemporary theological definitions of God, definitions that may well be worth discarding. Although the "God is dead" enthusiasts are modern Don Quixotes attacking windmills fabricated by well-meaning theologians, the value of the movement lies in the stimulation to study more practical ways and methods of applying eternal truths to contemporary problems and needs, without, however, compromising those truths.

A second denial of God's existence lies in the modern philosophy of science. There have supposedly occurred three eras in the civilization of man—the primitive age of superstition, the intermediate age of religion, and the present age of science. What was first explained in terms of superstition became comprehensible in terms of religion, to be finally replaced by the scientific exposition. God is supposedly no longer needed; his existence was postulated because of the ignorance of presently held scientific explanations of the nature of the world. However, closer examination of what in science is *fact* and what is *hypothesis* indicates that whatever truth has been scientifically demonstrated is perfectly compatible with the theological concept of the first cause. That is, science has found no evidence to contradict this theological truth, nor evidence to replace it.

A MEANINGLESS QUESTION?

For the logical positivist the problem of God's existence is a meaningless question. Indeed, for the positivist whatever cannot be adduced and verified quantitatively and experimentally is not admissible to the area of truth. It has been pointed out, however, that the positivistic premise is itself a philosophical position, not experimentally verifiable. It may be true that God is a meaningless subject for the positivist, but it does not follow that

God's existence *as such* is a meaningless issue. The positivistic position is an arbitrary one, assumed by those investigators who place reliance on the experimental method alone. It does not follow that matters which do not interest the positivist have for that reason no significance. All that a positivist can say is, "I am not interested." He cannot say, "My position does not admit such issues; therefore, such issues are meaningless and should be discarded."

EXISTENCE AND NATURE

It has been said that Herbert Spencer, the English philosopher, pointed out that inexorable logic proves the existence of God, but since he (Spencer) could not understand God's nature, he felt compelled to reject Him.

This view exemplifies the height of intellectual pride and is a grave error for either philosopher or scientist. The assumption that man should accept as true only those things he can fully understand is an unnecessary one. No one fully understands the nature of gravity or of energy. Yet these phenomena are accepted as part of reality. The *existence* of a truth should therefore be distinguished from the *nature* of a truth. God's existence can be proved by human reason, apart from questions regarding his nature.

Additional reasons relevant to the rejection of God can be found in previous chapters on the discussion of absolute certitude, the distinction between mind and brain, the treatment of religious maturity, and wherever impediments to human reason are evaluated in this book.

A FINAL NOTE

It should be observed that the *acceptance* of God's reality will not be effected by logic alone. In the final analysis, a personal experience of the existence of God is required. This chapter has attempted only to point out the reasonableness of his existence and the unreasonableness of opposing views. The personal relationship between God and man will be discussed in the chapters to follow, wherein faith will be seen to be the key to conviction.

Chapter 13

Morality, Conscience, and Sexuality

The perplexity in contemporary moral relations among nations, communities, and individuals is partially attributable to confusion on how human relationships should be conducted. What is the norm by which good
or bad morality is to be judged? Is there a norm universally applicable to
human conduct, or can there only be a multiplicity of standards, differentially binding in the numerous societies and cultures?

There are two mutually exclusive alternatives concerning the question of
what the standards of human moral conduct should be. The first alternative
is that of an absolute norm, binding universally on all men, regardless of
culture. The opposing option is that of a nonabsolute, or relative, state of
affairs, wherein moral standards would be a function of the diversity of
social structure. Let it be assumed for the moment that the latter alternative should be adopted.

RELATIVE NORMS OF MORALITY

The relativistic, or pragmatic, point of view is immediately faced with the
question as to the basis for a moral code. Should moral standards be based
on what man *does* or on what he *ought* to do? One relativistic position

rejects *a priori* standards for moral obligations and advocates *a posteriori* standards, based on an analysis of how man behaves in fact. Therefore, from an empirical point of view, the "ought" should be predicated on the "does." This trend is exemplified by the Kinsey report on human sexual behavior. Information on average sexual behavior can be used as a basis of determining what is good (desirable) and what is bad (undesirable) concerning sexual behavior. However, it also follows that man rapes, kills, cheats, steals, and lies, and average behavior statistics can also be computed in these areas. The fallacy of the use of the statistical average as a norm to dictate what is good or desirable in behavior has been previously discussed in the chapter on the criteria of healthy adjustment (Chapter 10). The average can be concluded to be a poor standard against which to measure desirable behavior.

If, then, the "ought" of behavior requires standards other than actual behavior, what are these standards to be? The "ought" of the atheistic mentality is not the same as that of the Christian. The "ought" of the Oriental mind is greatly different from that of the European intellect. Who is to decide the correct moral point of view? It should be obvious that moral law relative to the human mind is ultimately reduced to human opinion. And who is to decide which human opinion is superior to another? Relativism cannot dictate which human theory is correct without slipping into an absolutist position. Consequently, the reasonable opinion of any person, as opinion, is no better than anyone else's. Even the pragmatic tempering tool of empirical utilitarianism has its fault, because who is to decide what is useful and practical in moral conduct and what is not? The ultimate logical consequence of a relative moral law is moral chaos (Bourke, 1951).

AN ABSOLUTE NORM

The only alternative to a relative norm is one that is absolute. Obviously, the human mind is incapable of creating such a norm, which must be based on a perfect and complete understanding of human nature. Therefore, it is clear that the possibility of an absolute norm presupposes the existence of God, for only the Creator of man is in a position to dictate what is to be universally and absolutely binding on all men, regardless of differences in culture and civilization. That he has done so will be discussed in the chapters to follow, in which his self-communication to man will be examined.

HUMAN LIBERTY AND AN ABSOLUTE NORM

What bearing does an absolute moral norm have on human liberty? Does such a norm remove the traditional American freedoms of speech, religion, and the press? First, what is meant by *freedom*? Freedom, from the Christian point of view, means liberty *within* law, not liberty *from* law. Freedom from law or without law is not freedom at all, but rather lawlessness and license. Rights and duties are correlative (Bittle, 1950). With the right of liberty goes the duty of using such liberty properly. Thus, *freedom of speech* is freedom to speak as one should, not as one pleases. Slander, lies, malicious gossip, and knowingly false statements are morally evil abuses of liberty of speech. Similarly, *freedom of the press* does not include intrusion upon personal privacy, unless the common welfare demands such intrusion. Newspaper photographs of personal grief, e.g., a mother's agonized expression at the scene of a child's accidental death, cannot be justified as freedom of the press; they serve only the motive of sensationalism.

Again, from a Christian point of view, *freedom of religion* does not mean the freedom to deny the existence of God (since his existence is a reality), nor the freedom not to render him worship, but rather the freedom to worship God as one ought. An absolute moral law, being founded upon and receiving its validity from God, precludes any denial of the reality of its origin.

The demands of an absolute moral law might seem at first to present affronts to human liberty. However, human acceptance of such a code becomes reasonable when the difference between objective and subjective morality is understood.

OBJECTIVE AND SUBJECTIVE MORALITY

What has been discussed to this point regarding the absolute demands of the moral law can be designated *objective morality*. However, the acceptance and implementation of this law in human behavior is contingent on the individual human conscience and the individual's understanding of the moral law. A person's perception of what is expected of him by God can be termed *subjective morality*. The moral law includes the principle that implementation of the "ought" is tempered by a person's understanding and interpretation of the moral law. *Conscience* can be defined as (*a*) the intellectual discernment between moral right and moral wrong, together with (*b*) the realization that one should do what is perceived to be morally good and to avoid what is perceived to be morally evil and (*c*) the awareness of guilt after a moral transgression. One is always obligated to follow the intellectual light of one's own conscience, even in those instances when conscience dictates a course of action contrary to the objective demands of the moral law! A look at the various instances in which discrepancies arise between conscience and the moral law is now in order.

CONSCIENCE AND THE MORAL LAW

There are various dimensions of conscience to be considered in connection with the application of the moral law in human behavior (Figure 14).

A conscience can be considered to be true, *objectively speaking*, when it conforms with objective moral truth. For example, the recognition of the moral obligation to worship God as one's creator and ultimate end reflects a true conscience. An atheistic person, objectively speaking, has a false conscience.

Subjectively speaking, the atheist, for example, may be either certain or doubtful of the validity of his moral position (Figure 14). If he is certain, then he is innocent of the objective falsity of his condition. Indeed, he is obliged to follow his conviction, even though objectively it is in error, since one is always obliged to follow conscience if the conviction upon which it

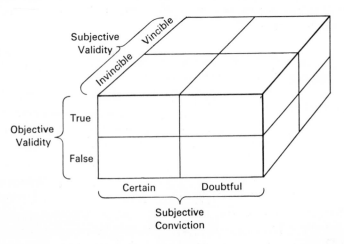

FIG. 14. Dimensions of conscience.

rests is experienced as certain. A doubtful conscience should ordinarily not be followed, whether it be Christian or non-Christian. The doubt should be clarified before moral action follows (Alexander, 1957).

Lastly, the state of conscience can be described as vincible or invincible (Figure 14). The opportunity for enlightenment leaves an ignorant conscience no excuse for ignorance, and such a conscience prior to available education can be viewed as vincible. An invincible conscience is exemplified in the person living beyond the reach of Christian civilization, a person who is not only ignorant of divine revelation but invincibly so.

OBLIGATIONS OF CONSCIENCE

As noted, one is morally obligated to follow the dictates of a certain conscience, whether it be true or false. A secondary obligation is to educate oneself in moral matters. A deliberate attempt to maintain moral ignorance increases rather than decreases moral culpability.

Since there obviously exist cultural differences in moral training, the next issue is the effect of culture on conscience.

CONSCIENCE AND CULTURE

Does culture form conscience? Certainly the mores recognized to be binding differ from one society to another. The content, or subject matter, of conscience is obviously learned. One is not born with the Ten Commandments written on one's conscience. However, even though moral information as such must be acquired, there are nonetheless three innate universal characteristics of conscience. The first is the intellectual capability of discerning the difference between right and wrong, regardless of what is considered to be right or wrong. Secondly, there is the universal recognition that one should follow the dictates of one's conscience. And lastly, there is the universal experience of guilt when one has transgressed one's conscience. These three functions of conscience are intellectual operations, and therefore universally experienced by all men, irrespective of culture or geography.

Therefore, conscience is partly innate (intelligence) and partly acquired (culture). The Christian further contends that one should educate conscience and seek God's will with respect to moral obligations. The personal application of God's revealed law to moral behavior is a continuing challenge to man.

THE CONTEMPORARY VIEWPOINT ON SEX

Chastity and modesty are virtues unlikely to be widely practiced, or held in high esteem, by the modern world. *Chastity* refers to purity in thought or deed, and *modesty* is the expression of this purity in attire. Chastity and modesty are ignored, even despised, in contemporary society. With regard to feminine apparel, newspaper advertisements and television commercials border on vulgarity. Modesty is flouted by modern-day styles for beach, street, and evening wear. The greatest rejection of these virtues, however, occurs in the entertainment milieu, in movies, plays, magazines, and publications.

It is difficult to know whether the public entertainment media reflect or determine the thinking of the times, or to know the extent of the interaction. Statistical studies on social behavior indicate that the American social pattern has deviated widely from its Judeo-Christian heritage. College campus sexual behavior, as well as that in the community, has become free of moral censure. The only control governing such behavior today is fear, the fear of possible pregnancy. Even this fear, however, is becoming attenuated by the availability to the unmarried of birth-control pills and access to abortionists.

The influence of the modern-day sex philosophy has pervaded both high-school and grade-school populations. Kissing games, all-night dances, weekend house parties, all contribute to occasions of sexual promiscuity. Necking, petting, and intercourse are no longer forbidden pleasures. Such behavior is tolerated by many parents who either have adopted contemporary moral standards, or have resigned themselves to social pressures on their teenage children.

THE NEW MORALITY

Sexual permissiveness and other non-Christian behavioral practices, e.g., psychedelic drug experimentation, have been embraced by a movement known as the "new morality." This movement seems to crystallize the contemporary revolt against an absolute standard of morality. The individual is free to do as he pleases, as long as no one is hurt, and "hurt" is defined only in terms of physical consequences, such as pregnancy, with total exclusion of any moral hurt, that is, sin.

There are four classes of individuals following the contemporary philosophy of sex. First, there are those who believe unrestricted sexual behavior to be wrong, yet rationalize their indulgence. The excusing situation may be varied. For example, when a city is liberated from the enemy, do not the heroes merit the special favors of the female population? Or, when a football foe is defeated, does the event not justify the students' indulgence in uninhibited sexual release? Or, as long as one's spouse and children are provided for, can one not justify an occasional extramarital fling? If conscience still agitates, there is the rationalizing solution of first becoming inebriated, for how can one be held responsible for behavior occurring in a state of drunkenness?

The second type of person implementing contemporary standards of sexuality is the hypocrite, one who pretends to be Christian but in reality does not behave as one, and in his conscience knows it.

The third class is the non-Christian who attempts to flee the problems of reality and the meaning of human existence through abandonment to sexual pleasure. Lastly, there is the individual who utilizes sex for personal gain, exemplified by the movie-maker and the magazine publisher who profit from pornography, either in the form of cheap magazines or in the more socially accepted guise of "sophisticated" publications for men.

THE CHRISTIAN CONCEPT OF SEX

Sex, according to the Christian viewpoint, is intimately related to the married life rather than to the single life. Sex provides for the completion of God's plan for procreation, as well as fulfillment of the physical expression of mutual love between man and wife. "God created man in his image. In the image of God he created him. Male and female he created them. Then God blessed them and said to them, 'Be fruitful and multiply; fill the earth and subdue it'" (Gen. 1:27–28). The pleasure of sex, created by God, is therefore good, sacred, wholesome. The proper use of this pleasure is even sanctifying. It is only the abuse that is evil. Similarly with all created goods; when used according to the Creator's intention, the relationship is lawful and good. When used contrary to his purpose, the relationship becomes unlawful and sinful.

God saw fit to give man two commandments concerning sexual behavior:

"You shall not commit adultery" and "You shall not covet your neighbor's wife" (Ex. 20:14, 17). In defining adultery, Our Lord declared, "You have heard that it was said to the ancients, Thou shalt not commit adultery. But I say to you that anyone who so much as looks with lust at a woman has already committed adultery with her in his heart" (Matt. 5:27-28). Therefore, to transgress this commandment, one need only have the desire to commit adultery. Those who persist in doing so shall not possess the kingdom of God (1 Cor. 6:9–10). St. Paul exhorts his brethren to follow nobly the way of purity: "For this is the will of God, your sanctification; that you abstain from immorality; that everyone of you learn how to possess his vessel in holiness and honor, not in the passions of lust like the Gentiles who do not know God..." (1 Thess. 4:3–5). "Flee immorality. Every sin that a man commits is outside the body, but the immoral man sins against his own body. Or do you not know that your members are the temple of the Holy Spirit, who is in you, Whom you have from God, and that you are not your own? For you have been bought at a great price. Glorify God and bear him in your body" (1 Cor. 6:18–20). St. Paul further warns,"... The Lord is the avenger of all these things, as we have told you before and have testified. For God has not called us to uncleanness, but unto holiness. Therefore, he who rejects these things rejects not man, but God, who has also given his Holy Spirit to us" (1 Thess. 4:6-8). St. Paul thus points out that immorality is an offense against God. Contrast this position with the contemporary view that there is no moral harm in sexual permissiveness.

It is difficult to lead a chaste life, particularly in a world that everywhere assaults the body with temptations to impurity. Yet God nevertheless expects man to be pure, even to become a saint. How? By cooperation with His grace. *On the natural level alone, it would be impossible to keep the commandments on sexual behavior; it is only with the supernatural help of God's grace that this accomplishment becomes possible.* When St. Paul feared succumbing to temptation, Our Lord said to him, "My grace is sufficient for thee, for strength is made perfect in weakness" (2 Cor. 12:9). With St. Paul, the Christian responds, "Gladly therefore I will glory in my infirmities, that the strength of Christ may dwell in me" (2 Cor. 12:9).

God has therefore promised the strength needed to fulfill his commandments. "And I will put my spirit in the midst of you, and I will cause you to walk in my commandments, and to keep my judgments and do them" (Ezech. 36:27). Our Lord himself declared, "Take my yoke upon you'.... For my yoke is easy, and my burden light" (Matt. 11:29, 30). Lastly, by way of encouragement, St. John writes, "For this is the love of God, that we keep his commandments; and his commandments are not burdensome. Because all that is born of God overcomes the world; and this is the victory that overcomes the world, our faith" (1 John 5:3–4).

The Christian, therefore, has a unique concept of sexuality, one incompatible with contemporary standards of morality. Yet the Christian should fight the good fight, that by his moral example the erring and the ignorant may become enlightened and no longer walk in the darkness of paganism.

Chapter 14

Suffering and Joy

The first part of this chapter will deal with psychological aspects of suffering and happiness, followed by a consideration of the orgin of evil in the world.

ON HAPPINESS

With reference to this topic the author has occasionally proposed three questions to his students, and the responses have been quite interesting. The first question is, Are you happy? The majority of students surprisingly responds in the negative. To the next question, Does the happiest part of your life lie in the past? the majority again replies in the negative. To the third question, Does the happiest part of your life lie in the future? the majority changes to an affirmative answer. The implication is clear. Most individuals feel that in neither the past nor the present have they satisfied their quest for happiness, yet they nourish the hope that such happiness will someday be realized.

The author, however, proposes a contrary hypothesis. It is this. If one is not happy *now*, at the present time of life, the chances are that one is not likely to be happy in the future either. Why not? For three reasons: the

153

great number of goals a person is capable of desiring, the restricted environmental opportunities to attain them, and the principle of adaptation. Let us examine the first two reasons, following the thought of T. V. Moore (1948).

In childhood, candy was not always forthcoming upon demand; in adolescence, recreational hours were restricted; in adulthood, there were insufficient funds to buy that new car; and in old age, there is the contention with aches and pains. Consequently, never will there be a time in life free of restrictions and limitations upon the attainment of desired goals. If one is not happy in the present, i.e., if one has not learned to adjust to the present frustrating environment, it would seem logical that one will not be happy in the future either. Now let us consider the third factor relating to happiness.

THE PRINCIPLE OF ADAPTATION

It is sometimes contended that those who are sufficiently wealthy to attain most worldly ambitions surely must be happier than those who lack such means. However, because of the principle of adaptation, this is a false observation. If, for example, one places a quarter in the palm of the hand, very shortly the pressure will no longer be felt. The hand has become pressure-adapted. Again, a newly purchased painting at first attracts the owner's eye whenever he enters the room. After a while, however, the painting is ignored. Adaptation has occurred.

Similarly, persons who possess material gain adapt after a time, and begin to cast acquisitive eyes at further or greater wealth. Even on the intellectual level the principle of adaptation applies. There is great satisfaction in obtaining the master's degree—until the opportunity for pursuing the Ph.D. degree becomes available. Therefore, no matter what ambitions are realized, the restless human spirit soon adapts and yearns for more. It is said that Alexander the Great wept because there were no more worlds to conquer.

If the reader still wishes he could at least have had the experience of adaptation to wealth, it should be considered that as an *experience* such adaptation had already been shared. The reader envying a neighbor's new car experiences the same kind of desire as the owner of a fifty-foot yacht gazing wistfully at his neighbor's hundred-foot yacht. Adaptation to one's present possessions is a universal phenomenon, experientially identical in all men.

Paradoxically, persons who divest themselves of material goods, e.g., religious aspirants who take a vow of poverty, can be the happiest people of all. Why? Because they need only to adapt to "nothing." Success in giving up the *desire* for personal possessions leaves one free of adaptation. Obviously, this is not an easy task, since there still exists the human tendency toward love of oneself, and the acquisition of things to serve that self-love. Therefore, an analysis of self-love, which initiates the acquisition of property, is next in order.

SELFISH AND UNSELFISH LOVE

Experience will testify that love of self creates an interminable search for self-satisfaction and self-service. It seems that the more the ego is gratified, the greater becomes the intensity of need for self-satisfaction, partially because of adaptation and partially because of the plenitude of desires cultivated by self-concern. In brief, the person who is totally ego-centered is the unhappiest person of all.

But there is another form of love, one that paradoxically combines life and death of self. This is the love of other-than-self, i.e., love of other people. Love of another person inevitably involves sacrifice, the denial of self-love. Indeed, in all times man has sought to communicate the proof of such love with a visible expression of self-sacrifice. The husband may work overtime in order to buy his wife an anniversary gift, the wife may spend many kitchen hours preparing a gourmet's delight for her husband, and a child may take special pains to draw a lovely valentine to give Mommy. Young lovers often display the most obvious expression of self-sacrifice, as each attempts to exceed the other's proof of love.

Such love, since it opposes self-love, is called *un*selfish. Psychologically, a death is involved. Unselfish love by nature demands a denial of the ego, for the sake of the other. This kind of love, however, brings through death a vitalization that is the essence of life. True living is true loving, and vice versa. Unselfish love, therefore, is the secret ingredient of true happiness. Happiness and joy in human existence are experienced in proportion to the degree that unselfish love is achieved. The more one learns to love unselfishly, the greater will be the happiness in one's life. The opposite is also true. For the drunkard or unfaithful spouse who loves himself more than his family, or for the quarrelsome person who loves his own will more than that of others, unhappiness begins when love is turned inward toward the satisfaction of selfish desires. Thus, one mystery of Scripture is psychologically as well as spiritually meaningful in the statement that one who wishes to save his life will lose it, and one who loses his life will find it.

True happiness in this life, therefore, consists of unselfish love. The spiritual significance of this psychological fact will be further developed in the chapters to follow.

THE ORIGIN OF EVIL

Even though one can learn to experience true happiness through love and service to others, there still remains the reality of suffering as part of everyone's life. Whether mental or physical, suffering, pain, and death are facts of life demanding resolution with the basic natural striving for self-preservation. Why this opposition? Whence came such evil? Philosophers have written an endless number of books on the subject of evil. In all instances the same answer is reached—suffering and death are unreasonable, cannot be explained rationally, and can be accepted only as part of the reality in which we find ourselves. It is true that human reason alone cannot explain the origin or meaningfulness of evil; the answer must be sought in divine revelation.

Evil can be defined negatively as the absence of good. Whenever a proper relationship is disturbed, the consequent distortion is known as evil. The Christian concept of evil places its origin at the time of creation of the angels. Some of these spiritual creatures rebelled against God and were punished. "And there was a battle in heaven; Michael and his angels battled with the dragon, and the dragon fought and his angels. And they did not prevail, neither was their place found any more in heaven. And that great dragon was cast down, the ancient serpent, he who is called the Devil and Satan, who leads astray the whole world; and he was cast down to the earth and with him his angels were cast down" (Rev. 12:7–9). Again, "Behold they that serve him are not steadfast, and in his angels he found wickedness" (Job 4:18). "And the angels also who did not preserve their original state, but forsook their abode, he has kept in everlasting chains under darkness for the judgment of the great day" (Jude 1:6). "How art thou fallen from heaven, O Lucifer, who didst rise in the morning? How art thou fallen to earth, that didst wound the nations?" (Isa. 14:12). Our Divine Lord himself referred to the angelic fall, "I was watching Satan fall as lightning from heaven" (Luke 10:18).

Satan, the leader of the fallen angels, was responsible for the temptation of Adam and Eve (Gen. 3:1–24), whose capitulation established the presence of ignorance, sin, suffering, and death in the world, all of which constituted mankind's punishment for rebellion against his Creator.

SATAN IN THE WORLD

The fallen angels have since plagued mankind in the attempt to lure others to share their unhappy lot. Satan was even so arrogant as to tempt Christ. "Again, the devil took him to a very high mountain, and showed him all the kingdoms of the world and the glory of them. And he said to him, 'All these things I will give thee, if thou wilt fall down and worship me'" (Matt. 4:8–9). Although rebuffed by Christ, devious Satan has succeeded with mortal man through the ages, and is still at work today. "Be sober, be watchful! For your adversary the devil, as a roaring lion goes about seeking someone to devour. Resist him, steadfast in the faith, knowing that the same suffering befalls your brethren all over the world" (1 Pet. 5:8–9). In contemporary society, the strongest assistance to Satan's work is the denial of his existence, for the greatest enemy is the unknown enemy.

GOD AND EVIL

It would at first appear very difficult to reconcile the existence of evil with the goodness of God. However, it must be remembered that man's present plight was not initially intended by God, but occurred through man's free decision to rebel against God. God, respecting man's free will, did not interfere with this decision. However, he did take pity on man, and in the same sentence of expulsion from Eden, promised salvation. (See Chapter 15.)

Our inheritance of Adam and Eve's sin can also be reconciled with God's justice. Adam and Eve can be considered, statistically speaking, a true and valid representative sample of all men and women. That is, if we were the ones tempted, rather than Adam or Eve, the consequences would have been the same. In other words, the strength and weakness of all of us were represented at their moment of temptation. In a sense, then, all mankind shared in original sin. Another interpretation is that original sin consists of the situation-state involving the sins of all mankind, into which each is born by virtue of being a member of the human race. This state is in later life ratified by personal sin (Schoonenberg, 1965).

SUFFERING SANCTIFIED

Not only did God redeem man; he chose to do so through the path of suffering. (See Chapters 15, 16.) God thereby sanctified suffering and pain, giving an example that we might do likewise. "And bearing the cross for himself, he went forth to the place called the Skull, in Hebrew, Golgotha, where they crucified him..." (John 19:17–18). To many, this example was foolish. "For the doctrine of the cross is foolishness to those who perish, but to those who are saved, that is, to us, it is the power of God... for the Jews ask for signs, and the Greeks look for 'wisdom,' but we, for our part, preach a crucified Christ—to the Jews indeed a stumbling-block and to the Gentiles foolishness" (1 Cor. 1:18, 22–23). The Christian, therefore, is expected to shoulder the cross. "If anyone wishes to come after me, let him deny himself, and take up his cross daily, and follow me. For he who would save his life will lose it; but he who loses his life for my sake will save it" (Luke 9:23–24; Matt. 16:24–25). "And he who does not take up his cross and follow me, is not worthy of me" (Matt. 10:38).

Acceptance of God's will in regard to pain and suffering is an intellectual decision, not an emotional one. Human nature has a distaste, even a dread, of pain. Christ himself begged release from the suffering he foresaw in Gethsemane. "'Father, if thou art willing, remove this cup from me; yet not my will but thine be done.' And there appeared to him an angel from heaven to strengthen him. And falling into an agony he prayed the more earnestly ..." (Luke 22:42–44).

It is the hope of the Christian to become, by God's grace, as zealous as the apostles. St. Paul lists the sufferings he has endured for love of Christ—lashes, prison, stoning, shipwreck, robbers, hunger and cold, and betrayal by brethren (2 Cor. 11:23–30). He later reveals his love of the cross. "But as for me, God forbid that I should glory save in the cross of our Lord Jesus Christ, through whom the world is crucified to me, and I to the world" (Gal. 6:14).

Our Divine Lord gave assurance of help in times of pain and trial. "Come to me, all you who labor and are burdened, and I will give you rest. Take my yoke upon you, and learn from me, for I am meek and humble of heart; and you will find rest for your souls. For my yoke is easy, and my burden light" (Matt. 11:28–30). "Peace I leave with you, my peace I give to you; not as the world gives do I give to you. Do not let your heart be troubled, or be afraid" (John 14:27).

The way of suffering has been marked by Our Savior, and made smooth by the steps of millions of good people before our time. The invitation is there to follow. By resignation to God's will, the ever-present reality of pain, and death, can become meaningful, fruitful, and a source of joy, in the knowledge of the eternal reward which awaits.

LOSS OF LOVED ONES

The greatest suffering that befalls man is brought by the death of one he loves. St. Paul summarizes the Christian attitude toward this reality of life. "Brethren, we would not have you lack understanding concerning those in the sleep of death, lest you yield to grief like the others, who have no hope. For if we believe that Jesus died and yet rose, so also will God bring forth with him those who have fallen asleep believing in Jesus. This we say to you as the Lord's own word, that we who live, who survive till the Lord's coming, will in no way have an advantage over those who have fallen asleep. No, for the Lord Himself, when the order is given, at the sound of Archangel's voice and of God's trumpet, will come down from heaven and the dead in Christ will first rise; then we the living, the survivors, will be caught up together with them in the clouds to meet the Lord in the air; and thus we shall be with the Lord always. Therefore, console one another with these words" (1 Thess. 4:13–18).

Christ's resurrection and triumph over death, and the profound significance of these events for man, will be discussed next.

Chapter 15

God and Man

Three approaches necessary for the adequate study of man have been proposed (Chapter 2). The third avenue of knowledge was defined as divine revelation, consisting of precepts communicated to man by God, for the reason that man by light of natural reason would never have arrived at their nature, their certainty, or their need. Faith was seen to be the human response necessary for acceptance of divine revelation. Before studying divine revelation, therefore, it would seem appropriate to analyze the concept of faith as a human experience.

FAITH

Faith in general embraces belief, trust, confidence, and conviction. There are two kinds of faith, human faith and divine faith. By human faith is meant man's trust in himself, his fellow man, and his environment. Faith in oneself may be psychological or physiological. We have confidence in our capabilities to think, reason, and make decisions. We trust our bodily functions to sustain physical life. A person also trusts his fellow man in daily affairs. We manifest such faith when depositing money in a bank, eating in public places, walking across busy intersections, or driving the expressways. One also exerts faith by communication with others, even by disagreements, wherein it is assumed the other party is honestly convinced of his opposition.

One also has confidence in one's environment. How often do we bother to be concerned about the possibility that oxygen might be eliminated from the atmosphere, or that a change in gravity might send us floating off into endless space. Faith, then, is seen to be a *natural human activity*, exerted by all people continuously throughout daily life, even by skeptics, who at least have faith in the validity of their skepticism. Moreover, the fact that human faith in oneself, others, or one's environment is occasionally betrayed does not detract from this activity as a natural human experience. In view of the foregoing evidence, faith in general is also seen to be a *reasonable human activity*.

Divine faith, too, embraces belief, trust, confidence, and conviction. This belief, however, is not placed in oneself, others, or the environment; rather, it rests in God himself. Divine faith consists of the belief in the validity of divine authority, together with the subsequent acceptance of truths divinely revealed. Rahner (1966) has described divine faith as surrender to the divine mysteries, and Kierkegaard has beautifully expressed it as a leap into the arms of God (Borzaga, 1966).

The reasonableness of divine faith as a human response rests first on the validity of the existence of God, which can be demonstrated. Conviction, however, flows from the personal experience of God. Secondly, the reasonableness of divine faith rests on the acknowledgment of man's finitude and the limitations of the human mind in its attempt to grasp absolute and ultimate knowledge. Although reasonable, divine faith should not be confused with reason. Reason is a natural function of the human intellect, and refers to truth comprehended by natural effort. Divine Faith starts where reason leaves off. For example, through reason the existence of God can be demonstrated, but it is only through divine faith that man can know and accept mysteries of God's nature, e.g., the Trinity, the Incarnation, or the Ten Commandments. Although divine faith complements reason, goes beyond reason, divine faith is not blind, as some critics would claim. Divine faith has its own illumination, a clarity of conviction that is immeasurably greater than the clarity of science or that of human reason. Here words fail, and only those who experience divine faith understand its nature. Lest this be construed as subterfuge, let it be understood that the *experience* of divine faith is within the grasp of those who would seek it.

TESTS OF FAITH

Human faith is tried when the object of our faith betrays our trust, whether that object be ourselves, others, or the environment. For example, we may choose unwisely (betrayed by ourselves), we may lose money invested in an ill-managed enterprise (betrayed by others), or we may be struck by lightning (betrayed by environment). The ratio of the number of experiences in which our human faith is confirmed to the number of experiences of betrayal will determine the strength or weakness of our human faith in ourselves, in others, or in our environment.

Divine faith, too, is tested by daily experience. Ordinary tests consist of temptations to ignore divine precepts, whether in the form of shirking positive commands (loving one's neighbor as oneself) or violating negative commands (theft, murder, adultery). Exceptional tests of divine faith are exemplified by occasions of tragedy, the loss of loved ones, or great loss of personal goods. Finally, there is the supreme test of divine faith when, at the time of one's own death, one's belief in personal resurrection is challenged.

Whether or not divine faith is sustained or lost is not just a function of the number of times of apparent betrayal. Authentic faith communicates the illumined conviction that the divine will is better than human will, that temporal disaster has meaning in an eternal perspective, that someday all things will be clear and understood, perhaps not in this life but certainly in the hereafter. Again, it should be noted that such a conviction is not blind, nor is it a desperate self-delusion or escape from reality. The illumination, assurance, and peace of authentic divine faith can be understood only by those who experience it.

COMPARISON OF HUMAN FAITH AND DIVINE FAITH

A contrast of human faith and divine faith may help in distinguishing their basic qualities. By way of similarity, both kinds of faith are reasonable, both are necessary human experiences, and both require the disposition of humility. Human faith is a reasonable and necessary experience in that such faith is required for normal peace of mind and implementation of daily life. Divine faith is reasonable and necessary in that the ultimate purpose and destiny of man cannot be understood without it. Both kinds of faith require humility, the recognition that human nature is limited, and that man is insufficient by himself alone. Even on the natural level, his contingency forces him to rely on others and his environment for personal, social, and physical survival.

However, there are also essential differences between human faith and divine faith. First, human faith is a *natural* experience—in other words, it is understood by natural intelligence. Divine faith is a *supernatural* experience, understood by divine illumination rather than the natural light of intelligence. Secondly, human faith is a universal experience, whereas divine faith is not, if we are to judge by those who deny it. Thirdly, human faith is attainable by one's own efforts and choice. Divine faith, while sought by personal effort, can be granted only by divine prerogative, i.e., only God can grant man this gift, a gift beyond purely personal striving. Fourthly, human faith embraces natural truths discussed and understood by natural reason. Divine faith, on the other hand, embraces divine truths beyond the capability of natural human discovery and beyond the light of natural reason. Divine truths are communicated or revealed to man by God himself. With regard to the third characteristic of divine faith and the limitations of personal effort, let it be understood again that this gift is available to all who earnestly, honestly, and humbly seek it. The gift of divine faith is the consequence of divine love.

DIVINE FAITH AND MEN OF SCIENCE

It has been already noted (Chapter 2) that there can be no real conflict or contradiction among the valid truths proposed by science, philosophy, and religion. Each discipline is necessary for a complete and authentic understanding of man's nature. This position has been shared by many scientists of the past and the present, all of whom recognize the reasonableness and necessity of belief in God and belief in Divine revelation. Ian Barbour, in his excellent work *Issues in Science and Religion* (1966), gives examples of those who have in their own lives reconciled science with theology, e.g., Galileo, Descartes, Newton, and Boyle. This synthesis is appealingly presented in Lecomte du Noüy's *Human Destiny* (1947), Alexis Carrell's *Man the Unknown* (1935), and James Jeans' *The Mysterious Universe* (1931). Mason's *The Great Design* (1935) includes persuasive commentaries by such renowned scientists as R. G. Aitken, J. A. Crowther, H. Driesch, A. S. Eve, C. S. Gager, O. Lodge, E. W. MacBride, M. M. Metcalf, C. L. Morgan, and J. A. Thompson. Arthur Compton's *The Human Meaning of Science* (1940) and C. A. Coulson's *Science and Christian Belief* (1955) are also commendable. Richard Bube's recent work *The Encounter Between Christianity and Science* (1968) is recommended as a current statement in this area.

These are but a few of the noteworthy volumes written by scientists who see divine faith unthreatened by the contemporary homage paid to science. Moreover, these authors realize the limitations of science and its proper role as one approach in the search for knowledge. It is neither the best nor the exclusive road to truth.

DIVINE REVELATION AND THE ULTIMATE PURPOSE OF MAN

It has been seen from a *philosophical* point of view that the ultimate end of man can be determined only negatively, that is, complete happiness and security cannot be attained in this life (Chapter 7). *Theologically*, however, a positive conclusion can be reached. It is the purpose of the rest of this chapter to present the contribution of divine revelation to the psychological study of man's entire personality, one vital aspect of which is spiritual fulfillment. Indeed, here is found the very essence, or core, of the human person. An individual's spiritual value system, whether it be Christian or non-Christian, has a profound effect on relationships with other men and with himself. The three primary and ultimate questions, Where did one come from? Why is one here? and Where is one going? demand resolution. The answers will bring either perpetual unhappiness or eternal joy, and behavior consequent to these decisions can completely transform the human personality.

SCRIPTURE

It is the Christian conviction that God spoke to man through men. These men were called prophets. Much of their inspiration they wrote down, resulting in a body of literature that is an essential part of Scripture. The credentials of these men rested on their miraculous powers and control over nature, a capability they could have received only from the Author of Nature. God thus formed a covenant, or testament, with mankind, in preparation for the time at which he would eventually become incarnate himself, and as a man, the God-Man, fulfill the entirety of divine revelation in the personality of Jesus Christ (Abbott, 1966).

But to understand the reason for this Incarnation of God, it is necessary to go back to the beginning of time, when man was first created.

CREATION AND REDEMPTION

The very first chapter of Scripture describes the creation of the world and lastly, of man. God, in his goodness and wisdom, willed to create a being in his own image, a creature to share his divine life, in the sense of possessing grace, intelligence, freedom, and bodily integrity. However, man violated his powers, disobeyed God, and was punished by the removal of certain preternatural gifts. He not only became subject to ignorance, concupiscence, sickness, and death, but also lost the heritage of living with God eternally. A question could be introduced here with regard to the reference of Scripture to Adam, the first man. Has mankind descended from a unique couple, Adam and Eve, or do Adam and Eve represent creation of man in plurality? The first point of view has been termed *monogenism* and the second *polygenism* (Francoeur, 1965; Donceel, 1965a). The scientific term equivalent to *polygenism* is *monophylism*, the position that mankind arose from a single phylum in the process of evolution. Which version is true will probably never be solved on either the scientific or the philosophical level. The final answer will rest on the correct interpretation of divine revelation.

In the same act of punishing man, God promised redemption, a reestablishment of the proper relationship between himself and man. The story of how God planned to do this is written in the Old Covenant, or Old Testament. Finally, following ages of yearning for the restoration of God's friendship, the moment arrived, marked in time as an event occurring some two thousand years ago. God took on human flesh, became man, and walked the earth in the person of Jesus Christ. At long last God now spoke directly to man, and clarified human origin, purpose, and destiny. No longer would there be any necessity for ignorance or confusion. Man's path would now be clearly marked, his destiny unmistakably known.

The mission of Jesus Christ, God the Son, was also revealed. That mission was his own death, by which a divine apology was to be made to God the Father for man's original sin. This death would once again admit man into the eternal presence of God. Why God chose such a drastic means of restoring man to his original purpose and destiny is a mystery of divine love. It can be accepted, and appreciated, only through the gift of faith.

CHRISTOLOGY AND EVOLUTION

Rahner (1966) relates the Incarnation to the evolution of man. The Incarnation marks the necessary and permanent beginning of the divinization of the world as a whole. In the Incarnation God took hold of the world and divinized matter, in the personality of Christ. God thus communicated himself to the world, and men must undergo a self-transcendence in order to accept this communication, to which they can close themselves only by guilt.

Concurrent with this interpretation is the concept of the Incarnation as being God's primary intention (and climax) in creating the cosmos, with the redemption of man as a secondary intention (Rahner, 1966).

THE INCARNATION OF CHRIST

St. John opens his gospel with the beautiful and mysterious words concerning the coming of God upon earth. "In the beginning was the Word, and the Word was with God; and the Word was God. He was in the beginning with God. All things were made through him, and without him was made nothing that has been made. In him was life, and the life was the light of men. And the light shines in the darkness; and the darkness grasped it not.... It was the true light that enlightens every man who comes into the world. He was in the world, and the world was made through him, and the world knew him not. He came unto his own, and his own received him not. But to as many as received him he gave the power of becoming sons of God; to those who believe in his name: who were born not of blood, nor of the will of the flesh, nor of the will of man, but of God. And the Word was made flesh, and dwelt among us. And we saw his glory—glory as of the only-begotten of the father—full of grace and of truth" (John 1:1–5, 9–14).

And thus the yearning of Isaiah was fulfilled, "Drop down dew, ye heavens, from above, and let the clouds rain the just; let the earth be opened, and bud forth a Savior..." (Isa. 45:8).

The Incarnation was the consequence of God's love for man. "For God so loved the world that he gave his only-begotten Son, that those who believe in him may not perish, but may have life everlasting" (John 3:16). And, "When the fullness of time came, God sent his son, born of a woman..." (Gal. 4:4).

Isaiah prophesied the birth of Christ. "For a Child is born to us, and a

Son is given to us, and the government is upon his shoulder; and his name shall be called Wonderful, Counsellor, God the Mighty, the Father of the world to come, the Prince of Peace" (Isa. 9:6). "Behold, a virgin shall conceive, and bear a son, and his name shall be called Emmanuel" (Isa. 7:14). The name Emmanuel is interpreted as "God with us."

And finally this event of love took place. "And there were shepherds in the same district living in the fields and keeping watch over their flock by night. And behold, an angel of the Lord stood by them and the glory of God shone round about them, and they feared exceedingly. And the angel said to them, 'Do not be afraid, for behold, I bring you good news of great joy which shall be to all the people; for today in the town of David a Savior has been born to you, who is Christ the Lord. And this shall be a sign to you: you will find an infant wrapped in swaddling clothes and lying in a manger.' And suddenly there was with the angel a multitude of the heavenly host praising God and saying, 'Glory to God in the highest, and peace among men of good will!'" (Luke 2:8–14).

THE REDEMPTION BY CHRIST

Although Satan succeeded in tempting Adam and Eve, God foretold Satan's failure to keep man captive. "I will put enmity between you and the woman, between your seed and her seed; he shall crush your head, and you shall lie in wait for his heel" (Gen. 3:15).

The earthly beginning of the salvation of man is beautifully narrated by St. Luke. "Now in the sixth month the angel Gabriel was sent by God to a town of Galilee called Nazareth, to a virgin betrothed to a man named Joseph, of the house of David, and the virgin's name was Mary. And when the angel had come to her, he said, 'Hail, full of grace, the Lord is with thee. Blessed art thou among women.' And when she had heard him she was troubled at his word, and kept wondering what manner of greeting this might be. And the angel said to her, 'Do not be afraid, Mary, for thou hast found grace with God. Behold, thou shalt conceive in thy womb and shalt bring forth a son; and thou shalt call his name Jesus. He shall be great, and shall be called the Son of the Most High, and the Lord will give him the throne of David his father, and he shall be king over the house of Jacob forever; and of his kingdom there shall be no end.' But Mary said to the angel, 'How shall this happen, since I do not know man?' And the angel an-

swered and said to her, 'The Holy Spirit shall come upon thee and the power
of the Most High shall overshadow thee; and therefore the Holy One to be
born shall be called the Son of God!... But Mary said, 'Behold the hand-
maid of the Lord; be it done to me according to thy word.' And the angel
departed from her'" (Luke 1:26–35, 38).

THE DIVINITY OF CHRIST

Jesus Christ claimed to be the Son of God. Indeed, it was this claim that
furnished the basis of his enemies' hate. "Not for a good work do we stone
thee, but for blasphemy, and because thou, being a man, makest thyself
God" (John 10:33). The charge arose again at his trial before Pilate. "We
have a Law, and according to that Law he must die, because he has made
himself Son of God" (John 19:7). And finally when Christ faced Caiphas,
the latter challenged, "'... I adjure thee by the living God that thou tell us
whether thou art the Christ, the Son of God.' And Jesus answered, 'Thou
hast said it. Nevertheless I say to you, hereafter you shall see the Son of
Man sitting at the right hand of the Power and coming upon the clouds of
heaven.' The high priest became enraged, and tore his garments, saying,
'He has blasphemed; what further need have we of witnesses. Behold, we
have heard the blasphemy'" (Matt. 26:63–65).

Christ also came to found a kingdom. "Pilate therefore again entered the
praetorium, and he summoned Jesus, and said to him, 'Art thou the king of
the Jews?'... Jesus answered, 'My kingdom is not of this world' ... Pilate
therefore said to him, 'Thou art then a king?' Jesus answered, 'Thou sayest
it; I am a king. This is why I was born, and why I have come into the world,
to bear witness to the truth. Everyone who is of the truth hears my voice!'"
(John 18:33, 36–37).

Jesus supported his claim to divinity by miracles. At least thirty-five are
detailed in the Gospels, and others are described in general (Vaughan,
1957; Alexander, 1954). For example, he changed water into wine (John
2:1–11), stilled a storm at sea (Matt. 8:23–27), healed the blind (Matt.
9:27–31, John 9:1–41, Mark 8:22–26, Matt. 20:29–34), multiplied loaves
and fishes (Luke 9:12–17, Matt. 15:32–39), and raised the dead to life
(Matt. 9:23–26, Luke 7:11–16, John 11:11–44). His greatest miracle, however, was his own resurrection (Matt 28:1–15, Mark 16:1–13, Luke 24:1–
12, 33–35, John 20:1–31).

THE HUMILITY OF CHRIST

As Adam had sinned through pride and disobedience, Christ made reparation through humility and obedience. ". . . Christ Jesus, who though he was by nature God, did not consider being equal to God a thing to be clung to, but emptied himself, taking the nature of a slave and being made like unto men. And appearing in the form of man, he humbled himself, becoming obedient to death, even to death on a cross" (Phil. 2:5–8). Our Divine Lord himself exhorted, "Take my yoke upon you, and learn from me, for I am meek and humble of heart" (Matt. 11:29).

THE SUFFERINGS OF CHRIST

In the mystery of divine love, God the Son chose suffering as the means of redemption (Goodier, 1944; Hammes, 1964). The prophets visualized the torment of the Messiah. "My God, my God, why have you forsaken me, far from my prayer, from the words of my cry. O my God, I cry out by day, and you answer me not; by night and there is no relief for me'. . . But I am a worm, not a man; the scorn of men, despised by the people, All who see me scoff at me; they mock me with parted lips, they wag their heads: 'He relied on the Lord; let him deliver him, let him rescue him, if he loves him.' . . . Be not far from me, for I am in distress; be near, for I have no one to help me. Many bullocks surround me; the strong bulls of Basan encircle me. They open their mouths against me like ravening and roaring lions. I am like water poured out; all my bones are racked. My heart has become like wax melting away within my bosom. My throat is dried up like baked clay, my tongue cleaves to my jaws; to the dust of death you have brought me down. Indeed, many dogs surround me, a pack of evildoers closes in upon me; they pierced my hands and feet; I can count all my bones" (Ps. 21:2–3, 7–9, 12–17).

"Yet it was our infirmities that he bore, our sufferings that he endured, while we thought of him as stricken, as one smitten by God and afflicted. But he was pierced for our offenses, crushed for our sins; upon him was the chastisement that makes us whole, by his stripes we were healed. We had all gone astray like sheep, each following his own way; but the Lord laid upon him the guilt of us all. Though he was harshly treated, he submitted and opened not his mouth, like a lamb led to the slaughter or a sheep before the shearers, he was silent and opened not his mouth" (Isa. 53:4–7).

"Insult has broken my heart, and I am weak, I looked for sympathy, but there was none; for comforters, and I found none. Rather they put gall in my food, and in my thirst they gave me vinegar to drink" (Ps. 68:21–22).

The gospels bear eloquent testimony to these prophecies in the story of Jesus' passion and death (Matt. 26–28, Mark 14–16, Luke 22–24, John 13–21).

THE COMPASSION OF CHRIST

The suffering and death of Our Divine Lord, as well as his miraculous cures, are evidence enough for his compassion for mankind. There are, however, numerous other instances illustrating his compassion for the individual person. He wept at the death of his friend Lazarus (John 11:11–44), had pity on the widow of Naim (Luke 7:11–16), and yearned for the salvation of men. "Jerusalem, Jerusalem, thou who killest the prophets, and stonest those who are sent to thee! How often I would have gathered thy children together, as a hen gathers her young under her wings, but thou wouldst not" (Matt. 23:37, Luke 13:34).

Our Lord described himself as a shepherd. "I am the good shepherd, and I know mine and mine know me, even as the father knows me and I know the father; and I lay down my life for my sheep. And other sheep I have that are not of this fold. Them also I must bring, and they shall hear my voice, and there shall be one fold and one shepherd" (John 10:14–16).

When our Lord met the Samaritan woman at Jacob's well in Sichar, he spent considerable time conversing with her, speaking of spiritual water and eternal life. "Everyone who drinks of this water will thirst again. He, however, who drinks of the water that I will give him shall never thirst; but the water that I will give him shall become in him a fountain of water, springing up into life everlasting" (John 4:13–14). After further conversation, the woman inquired whether Christ could be the Messiah, and Jesus responded, "I who speak with thee am he" (John 4:26).

Jesus took pity on the weakness of Nicodemus, a Pharisee who visited him at night for fear of social ostracism. After explaining the necessity of spiritual rebirth, Our Divine Lord uttered the beautiful words of redemption, "For God so loved the world that he gave his only-begotten Son, that those who believe in him may not perish, but may have life everlasting" (John 3:16).

There is also the incident wherein Christ, after his Resurrection, appeared unrecognized to two of his followers (Luke 24:31–35). He inquired about their sadness, and when they told him of the death of their Master, he gently admonished them, "O foolish ones and slow of heart to believe in all the prophets have spoken! Did not the Christ have to suffer these things before entering into his glory?" (Luke 24:25–26). He then opened their hearts and minds with such words of inspiration that they asked him to tarry and have dinner with them. It was in the breaking of bread that their eyes were opened and they recognized him, whereupon"... he vanished from their sight" (Luke 24:31). The two disciples reproached themselves for not recognizing Jesus sooner. "Was not our heart burning within us while he was speaking on the road and explaining to us the Scriptures?" (Luke 24:32). And rising that very hour, they hastened back to Jerusalem, to relate the wonderful event to the other disciples.

CHRIST, THE BREAD OF LIFE

As a pledge of salvation, Our Divine Savior promised that he himself was to be the nourishment of man. "'For the bread of God is that which comes down from heaven and gives life to the world.' They said therefore to him, 'Lord, give us always this bread.' But Jesus said to them, 'I am the bread of life. He who comes to me shall not hunger, and he who believes in me shall never thirst'... Amen, amen, I say to you, he who believes in me has life everlasting. I am the bread of life. Your fathers ate the manna in the desert and have died. This is the bread that comes down from heaven, so that if anyone eat of it he will not die. I am the living bread that has come down from heaven. If anyone eat of this bread he shall live forever; and the bread that I will give is my flesh for the life of the world.'"

"The Jews on that account argued with one another, saying, 'How can this man give us his flesh to eat?' Jesus therefore said to them, 'Amen, amen, I say to you, unless you eat the flesh of the Son of Man, and drink his blood, you shall not have life in you. He who eats my flesh and drinks my blood has life everlasting and I will raise him up on the last day. For my flesh is food indeed, and my blood is drink indeed. He who eats my flesh and drinks my blood, abides in me and I in him ... He who eats this bread shall live forever'" (John 6:33–35, 47–57, 59).

Many hearing these words of Jesus did not understand how he would accomplish his declarations, and we read that"... from this time many of his disciples turned back and no longer went about with him. Jesus therefore said to the Twelve, 'Do you also wish to go away?' Simon Peter therefore answered, 'Lord, to whom shall we go? Thou hast words of everlasting life, and we have come to believe and to know that thou art the Christ, the Son of God'" (John 6:66–72). Even though Peter himself did not know how the Master would implement his pronouncement, he did not turn away in skeptic disbelief, but rather in a marvelous act of faith accepted this mystery.

The fulfillment of Christ's mystical promise occurred on the night he was to begin his passion and death. "And while they were at supper, Jesus took bread, and blessed and broke, and gave it to his disciples, 'Take and eat; this is my body.' And taking a cup, he gave thanks and gave it to them, saying, 'All of you drink of this; for this is my blood of the new covenant, which is being shed for many unto the forgiveness of sins'" (Matt. 26:26–28).

The wonderful privilege of this partaking of divinity has also the obligation of proper disposition. "For as often as you shall eat this bread and drink the cup, you proclaim the death of the Lord, until he comes. Therefore, whoever eats this bread or drinks the cup of the Lord unworthily, will be guilty of the body and the blood of the Lord" (1 Cor. 11:26–27).

CHRISTIANITY

The New Testament, or New Covenant, relates therefore the story of the new relation of God to man, in the person of Jesus Christ. During his lifetime, the divine Master gathered about him certain followers, whom he chose to continue and transmit his teachings to generations to come. Indeed, he commanded them to teach, to govern, and to sanctify. "... All power in heaven and earth has been given me. Go, therefore, and make disciples of all nations, baptizing them in the name of the Father, and the Son, and of the Holy Spirit, teaching them to observe all that I have commanded you; and behold, I am with you all days, even unto the consummation of the world" (Matt. 28:18–20). Interestingly enough, there is no evidence to indicate that he commanded any of his apostles to write, nor did he himself do so. That is why the New Testament, a compilation of what the apostles did eventually write down, is said to be but a partial expression of divine revelation. Indeed, St. John concludes his gospel with the interesting statement, "There are, however, many other things that Jesus did; but if every one of these should be written, not even the whole

world itself, I think, could hold the books that would have to be written"
(John 21:25). What the apostles learned from Christ, and taught, but which
they did not write down, is referred to as *sacred tradition*. Evidence of such
teaching is further supported by the early writings of the Church Fathers
during the first two hundred years of Christianity (Fremantle, 1953). St.
Paul himself urged the early Christians to hold fast to the traditions they
learned either by word of mouth or by letter (2 Thess. 2:15). Obviously, the
guarantee of the unchanged integrity of such oral tradition rests on the
guidance of the Holy Spirit, whom Jesus Christ promised to send for this
purpose (John 14:16–17, 16; Matt. 28:19).

THE HOLY SPIRIT

Although the three persons of the Trinity compose but one divine nature,
it is customary to attribute to each a function in the successive phases in the
development of mankind's relationship with God. God the Father is associated with creation, God the Son with redemption, and God the Holy
Spirit with guidance of the Church.

Prior to his death, our Divine Lord promised to send the Holy Spirit.
"If you love me, keep my commandments. And I will ask the Father and he
will give you another Advocate to dwell with you forever, the Spirit of truth
whom the world cannot receive, because it neither sees him nor knows him.
But you shall know him, because he will dwell with you, and be in you"
(John 14:15–17). "These things I have spoken with you while yet dwelling
with you. But the Advocate, the Holy Spirit, whom the Father will send in
my name, he will teach you all things, and bring to your mind whatever I
have said to you" (John 14:26). "But when the Advocate has come, whom
I will send you from the Father, the Spirit of Truth who proceeds from the
Father, he will bear witness concerning me" (John 15:26).

Subsequently, the Holy Spirit came upon the apostles on the day of Pentecost, and it was not until then that they had the courage to go forth and
preach Christianity. "And when the days of Pentecost were drawing to a
close, they were all together in one place. And suddenly there came a sound
from heaven, as of a violent wind blowing, and it filled the whole house
where they were sitting. And there appeared to them parted tongues as of
fire, which settled upon each of them. And they were all filled with the Holy
Spirit, and began to speak in foreign tongues, even as the Holy Spirit
prompted them to speak" (Acts 2:1–4).

And thus the apostles began the establishment of the Christian community throughout the world (Abbott, 1966). As St. Clement wrote about A.D. 100, "Christ was sent by God, the Apostles by Christ. They appointed bishops and deacons.... They made order that when they died, other men of tried virtue should succeed in their ministry" (Sheehan, 1949). And St. Irenaeus, around A.D. 150, discoursed on "... the bishops and their successors down to our time who have been appointed by the Apostles" (Sheehan, 1949). What, then, is expected of those who follow Christ? The significance of the personal meaning of God in man's life is our next and final topic of discussion.

Chapter 16

Unity With God

The Christian concept of the relationship of God to man is not cold and aloof. Rather, it stresses the personal contact with God, the singular experience of his love, concern, and solicitude for the individual's welfare, both spiritual and material.

THE MYSTICAL BODY OF CHRIST

Our Divine Lord spoke often of this personal union and mysterious identity that God wished to have with man.

"I am the true vine, and my Father is the vine-dresser. Every branch in me that bears no fruit he will take away; and every branch that bears fruit he will cleanse, that it may bear more fruit. You are already clean because of the word that I have spoken to you. Abide in me, and I in you. As the branch cannot bear fruit of itself unless it remain on the vine, so neither can you unless you abide in me. I am the vine, you are the branches. He who abides in me, and I in him, he bears much fruit; for without me you can do nothing. If anyone does not abide in me, he shall be cast outside as the branch and wither; and they shall gather them up and cast them into the fire, and they shall burn. If you abide in me, and if my words abide in you, ask whatever you will and it shall be done to you. In this is my Father glorified, that you may bear very much fruit, and become my disciples. As the Father has loved me, I have loved you. Abide in my love. If you keep my commandments you will abide in my love, as I also have kept my Father's commandments, and abide in his love. These things I have spoken to you that my joy may be in you, and that your joy may be full" (John 15:1–11).

"Yet not for these only do I pray, but for those also who through their word are to believe in me, that all may be one, even as thou, Father, in me and I in thee; that they also may be one in us, that the world may believe that thou hast sent me. And the glory that thou has given me, I have given to them, that they may be perfected in unity, and that the world may know that thou hast sent me, and that thou has loved them even as thou hast loved me" (John 17:20–23).

St. Paul experienced the identity God has with members of his Church. "And as he went on his journey, it came to pass that he drew near to Damascus, when suddenly a light from heaven shone round about him; and falling to the ground, he heard a voice saying to him, 'Saul, Saul, why dost thou persecute Me?' And he said, 'Who art Thou, Lord?' And He said, 'I am Jesus, Whom thou art persecuting . . .'" (Acts 9:3–5).

Realizing this doctrine, St. Paul teaches it to others. "For as the body is one and has many members, and all the members of the body, many as they are, form one, so also is it with Christ" (1 Cor. 12:12). "For in one Spirit we were all baptized into one body, whether Jews or Gentiles, whether slaves or free; and we were all given to drink of one Spirit.... But God has so tempered the body together in due portion as to give more abundant honor where it was lacking; that there may be no disunion in the body, but that the members may have care for one another. And if one member suffers anything, all the members suffer with it, or if one member glories, all the members rejoice with it. Now you are the body of Christ, member for member ..." (1 Cor. 12:12–13, 24–27). "One body and one Spirit, called to the same hope, one Lord, one faith, one baptism, one God and father of us all, who is above all, and throughout all, and in us all." (Eph. 4:6).

Theologically, the members of the church are therefore referred to as the Mystical Body of Christ, and the vitalizing force within this Body is the Holy Spirit (Abbott, 1966; Pius XII, 1943).

CHRISTOGENESIS

It was seen that within a world vision, evolution can be meaningfully related to the future spiritual development of man (Chapter 5). Man will not become God, the error of pantheism, but is to become more God-like. Only a personal, spiritual, immanent, and eternal focal point will satisfy the orthogenetic trend in the evolution of present society. Teilhard posits Christ as this Omega point, in reference to Him as the Alpha and Omega of the Apocalypse (Teilhard, 1965). This becoming-like-Christ, or *Christogenesis*, has always been the goal of the Christian (Rahner, 1966).

THE CHRISTIAN VOCATION

The privilege of membership in the Mystical Body of Christ has correlative duties. First, there is the obligation to live one's interior life in accordance with Christian teaching, as to ensure attainment of the blessed hope of eternal life with God. However, love of God embraces love of neighbor, and therefore the Christian should be equally concerned with the welfare of his fellow man, since all are members of one Body. Indeed, the behavior of the Christian as an individual has a spiritually resonating effect on the entire Mystical Body of Christ. To the extent that one lives a full Christian life, the spiritual progress of the Mystical Body is furthered, and to the extent that personal negligence exists, the Mystical Body is spiritually harmed. Christians therefore share in mankind's joy, sorrow, and spiritual progress, for all are united in Christ.

Paul speaks of the Christian's personal spiritual contribution to the Mystical Body: "I rejoice now in the sufferings I bear for your sake; and what is lacking of the sufferings of Christ I fill up in my flesh for his body, which is the Church" (Col. 1:24). Even though the death of Jesus Christ was of sufficient satisfaction for the sins of men and for the salvation of men, nonetheless the Christian by his personal effort aids in the *application* of Christ's merits to mankind.

LOVE FOR GOD

Man's love of God is still a human love, in that it usually has an emotional element, by analogy similar to the icing on a cake. The essence of love of

God, however, is not emotion, as the essence of the cake is not the icing. The love of God can be at times distasteful, or even painful. Consider for a moment Christ's human reaction in Gethsemane, when in bloody sweat he contemplated the suffering he would soon assume for the love of man. And at another time, our Lord declared, "Not every one who says Lord, Lord, shall enter the kingdom of Heaven, but he who does the will of my father" (Matt. 7:21), and, "If you love me, keep my commandments" (John 14:15).

Love of God involves humility, charity, and abandonment to the will of God (Boylan, 1954). It requires humility to accept one's own deficiencies, charity to accept those of others, and patience to resign oneself, particularly in times of tragedy, to the divine will. It is God who knows what is best, even though the human encounter with evil and suffering may not be understood, and may even appear unreasonable and unjust.

Keeping the commandments involves renunciation, not of one's fellow man, but of the snares of false and material values. St. John cautions against this danger. "Do not love the world, or the things that are in the world. If anyone loves the world, the love of the Father is not in him; because all that is in the world is the lust of the flesh, and the lust of the eyes, and the pride of life; which is not from the father, but from the world. And the world with its lust in passing away, but he who does the will of God abides forever" (1 John 2:15-17). St. Paul also urges the practice of Christian virtue. "Walk in the Spirit, and you will not fulfill the lusts of the flesh. For the flesh lusts against the spirit, and the spirit against the flesh; for these are opposed to each other, so that you do not do what you would. But if you are led by the Spirit, you are not under the Law. Now the works of the flesh are manifest, which are immorality, uncleanness, licentiousness, idolatry, witchcrafts, enmities, contentions, jealousies, anger, quarrels, factions, parties, envies, murders, drunkenness, carousings, and suchlike. And concerning these I warn you, as I have warned you, that they who do such things will not attain the kingdom of God. But the fruit of the Spirit is: charity, joy, peace, patience, kindness, goodness, faith, modesty, continency. Against such things there is no law. And they who belong to Christ have crucified their flesh with its passions and desires" (Gal. 5:16-24).

LIFE THROUGH DEATH

The Christian discovers eternal life through a temporal death. Let us look again at Our Lord's statement, "If anyone wishes to come after me, let him deny himself, and take up his cross, and follow me. For he who would save his life will lose it; but he who loses his life for my sake will find it" (Matt. 16:24–25). This death to sin and the world, with consequent life in Christ, is not possible by human effort unaided. It can be accomplished only by the gift of *sanctifying grace*, a spiritual strength given by God to achieve what would otherwise be humanly impossible.

It has already been pointed out that all love other than self- love involves sacrifice, a form of death. So also it is with love of God. But the world is still the environment in which we find ourselves, and in which we must learn to live. Our Lord asked his heavenly Father, "I do not pray that thou take them out of the world, but that thou keep them from evil" (John 17:15). Grace and strength are available; we need only to cooperate with God. Love, therefore, is the key to Christian perfection. Self-denial, sacrifice, penance for sin, suffering—all these become meaningful in the love for God. As human love, e.g., the love of parent for child or love between spouses, renders labor light, so does love of God overcome all. "Who shall separate us from the love of Christ? Shall tribulation, or distress, or persecution, or hunger, or nakedness, or danger, or the sword?... But in all these things we overcome because of him who has loved us. For I am sure that neither death, nor life, nor things present, nor things to come, nor powers, nor height, nor depths, nor any other creature will be able to separate us from the love of God, which is in Christ Jesus Our Lord" (Rom. 8:35, 37–39).

LOVE OF NEIGHBOR

Love of neighbor is inseparably bound with love of God (Merton, 1955). Our Lord said, "Thou shalt love the Lord thy God with thy whole heart, and with thy whole soul, and with thy whole mind. This is the greatest and the first commandment. And the second is like it, thou shalt love thy neighbor as thyself. On these two commandments depend the whole Law and the Prophets" (Matt. 22:37–40). Again, "A new commandment I give unto you: That you love one another, as I have loved you, that you also love one another. By this will all men know that you are my disciples, if you have love for one another" (John 13:34–35). "Greater love than this no man hath, that a man lay down his life for his friends" (John 15:13).

To love one's neighbor does not mean one must like one's neighbor, but rather that one wishes him well (Boylan, 1954). Love of neighbor here is supernaturally rather then naturally motivated. Obviously, it helps if one can learn to like others as well.

With supernatural love goes the willingness to forgive others' offenses. In the Lord's Prayer we pray "... Forgive us our debts, *as we forgive our debtors*" (Matt. 6:12). In the midst of his agony, Our Lord prayed, "... forgive them, father, for they know not what they do" (Luke 23:34). At another time, he admonished, "But I say to you, love your enemies, do good to those who hate you, and pray for those who persecute and calumniate you.... You are therefore to be perfect, even as your heavenly father is perfect" (Matt. 5:44, 48).

THE PERFECT CHRISTIAN

The model of the perfect follower of Christ, the one who loved and cherished him most, who suffered deeply in the witness of his rejection and crucifixion, is the Mother of Christ (Carol, 1956; Rahner, 1963). The close relation between Mary and Jesus has been acknowledged since the beginning of Christian civilization in the classical paintings, sculptures, and memorial churches of all ages. Famous artists of every era have felt the challenge to capture in color or in stone the mystical love between Mother and Son (Carol, 1961). Indeed, the great Michelangelo, believing he had succeeded where most fail, announced this victory by inscribing his name on his "Pietà," the only work bearing his signature.

The affection, respect, and honor that the Church bestows on Mary is not owing to mere reverence for motherhood. It is rather offered because God, in choosing her to clothe divinity in human flesh, making possible the Incarnation of the Word, has thereby bestowed on Mary a unique privilege never before or since known (Carol, 1956, 1957). God blessed Mary with a plentitude of grace and love, to strengthen her to fulfill the immense obligations of this profound privilege. She was not only to enjoy the wonderful experience of bringing Jesus into the world, to nourish him in infancy, and to guide his development in childhood; she was also to witness divinity spit upon, reviled, cursed, and crucified (Alphonsus de Liguori, 1931; Hammes, 1958, 1962). Her suffering was in proportion to her love, and therefore of tremendous depth (Raymond, 1954).

Examples of Mary's love of neighbor are found in scriptural narration of her concern for her cousin, Elizabeth (Luke 1:39–56), her solicitude at the Cana wedding, where she prompted her Divine Son to perform his first miracle (John 2:1–11), and in her maternal care of the disciples. However, it is Calvary that exemplifies the heights of her love of mankind, where she freely stood beneath the Cross (John 19:25) and generously cooperated in the sacrifice of her beloved Son (Carol, 1957).

The Church contends that Christ's gift of his Mother to St. John (John 19:26–27) is actually a gift to all men. As the spiritual mother of men, bringing forth her children in spiritual labor beneath the Cross, Mary has the greatest of all human love for men. Even today, in her heavenly home, Mary is still concerned with the welfare of her children, and earnestly desires that the sacrifice and sufferings of her Son be not in vain.

It is no wonder, then, that Christians through the ages have embraced Mary in their hearts, beholding her as the exemplar of the love and teachings of her Divine Son, and imitating her virtues in order to attain the fullness of the Christian life (Carol, 1955; Thomas à Kempis, 1954).

MAN'S FINAL GOAL

It has been seen in the chapter on man's final goal that absolute happiness and security are not to be found in this life, but rather beyond. God has chosen to reveal to man this fact. Our Lord told his disciples, "In my father's house there are many mansions. Were it not so, I would have told you, because I go to prepare a place for you. And if I go and prepare a place for you I am coming again, and I will take you to myself; that where I am, there you also may be" (John 14:2–3). St. John writes,"And God shall wipe away every tear from their eyes, and death shall be no more; neither shall there be mourning, nor crying, nor pain any more, for the former things have passed away" (Apoc. 21 :4).

Even if one were to spend a lifetime attempting to imagine the nature of this afterlife, it would be wasted effort, for "... eye has not seen nor ear heard, nor has it entered into the heart of man, what things God has prepared for those who love him" (1 Cor. 2:9). On the other hand, the loss of this heavenly existence must indeed constitute the nature of hell.

THE RESURRECTION

Although man must die, he will eventually be resurrected. Jesus told Martha, grieving over Lazarus' death, "I am the resurrection and the life:

he who believes in me, even if he die, shall live; and whoever lives and believes in me, shall never die" (John 11:25–26). And St. Paul consoles the bereaved with the following words. "But we would not, brethren, have you ignorant concerning those who are asleep, lest you should grieve, even as others who have no hope. For if we believe that Jesus died and rose again, so with him God will bring those also who have fallen asleep through Jesus ... and so we shall ever be with the Lord. Wherefore, comfort one another with these words" (1 Thess. 4:13–14, 17–18).

All great truths are simple, and the simplest of all truths can be stated in one sentence: man's purpose is to know and to love God in this life, and to be forever happy with him in the next. Whether or not the individual wishes to pursue this destiny is a personal decision, for paradoxically man has the freedom to rebel against the ultimate purpose for his existence. However, it is the hope and prayer of the Christian that all men search diligently for the will of God in their own lives, and fulfill that will in accordance with the light of an informed conscience.

In conclusion, it is the author's prayer for the reader that God "... may grant you from his glorious riches to be strengthened with power through his Spirit unto the progress of the inner man; and to have Christ dwelling through faith in your hearts: so that, being grounded in love, you may be able to comprehend with all the saints what is the breadth and length and height and depth, and to know Christ's love which surpasses knowledge, in order that you may be filled unto all the fullness of God" (Eph. 3:16–19).

PART IV   SUGGESTED READINGS

Abbott, W. M. (Ed.) *The documents of Vatican II*. New York: Herder, 1966. "The Church"; "The Church Today."

Alexander, A. F. *College moral theology*. Chicago: Regnery, 1957. Ch. 1. "Principles."

Alexander, A. F. *College apologetics*. Chicago: Regnery, 1954. Part I. "The Origin of Religion."

Altizer, T. *Toward a new Christianity—Readings in the death of God theology*. New York: Harcourt, Brace & World, 1967. Ch. 7. "Two Passages from *The Epistle to the Romans*" (Barth); Ch. 9. "Justification by Doubt and the Protestant Principle" (Tillich); Ch. 10. "Passages from *Theology of the New Testament*" (Bultmann); Ch. 14. "The Future of Christianity in a Post-Christian Era" (Vahanian); Ch. 15. "The New Essence of Christianity" (Hamilton); Ch. 16. "The Meaning of the Gospel, from *The Secular Meaning of the Gospel: Based on an Analysis of Its Language*" (Van Buren).

Barbour, I. G. *Issues in science and religion.* Englewood Cliffs: Prentice-Hall, 1966. Ch. 13. "God and Nature."

Barbour, I. *Christianity and the scientist.* New York: Association Press, 1960. Ch. 5. "Science and the Social Order"; Ch. 6. "The Scientist as a Person."

Barrett, W. *What is existentialism?* New York: Grove Press (paperback), 1964. Part I. "What Is Existentialism?"

Bittle, C. N. *Man and morals.* Milwaukee: Bruce, 1950. Ch. VI. "Man's Ultimate End"; Ch. VII. "The Norm of Morality"; Ch. XII. "Rights and Duties"; Ch. XIII. "God and Man."

Blackham, H. J. (Ed.) *Reality, man, and existence: Essential works of existentialism.* New York: Bantam Press (paperback), 1965. "An Introduction to Existentialist Thinking" (pp. 1–15).

Bourke, V. J. *Ethics.* New York: Macmillan, 1951. Ch. II. "The Purpose of Human Life"; Ch. VI. "Conscience and Moral Obligation"; Ch. XVI. "The Supernatural Life."

Boylan, M. E. *This tremendous lover.* Westminster, Md.: Newman, 1954. Ch. II. "The Plan of Restoration"; Ch. XX. "Confidence in Christ."

Breisach, E. *Introduction to modern existentialism.* New York: Grove Press (paperback), 1962. Part III, C: "The Religious Existentialists."

Bube, R. (Ed.) *The encounter between Christianity and science.* Grand Rapids: W. B. Eerdman, 1968. Ch. 2. "The Nature of Christianity" (Bube); Ch. 3. "Natural Revelation" (Bube); Ch. 10. "Social Science" (Moberg).

Buber, M. *Knowledge of man.* New York: Harper & Row (Torchbooks, paper), 1965. Ch. I. "Introductory Essay" (Friedman).

Buber, M. *I and thou.* New York: Scribner, 1958. "Part I."

Cavanagh, J. R., and McGoldrick, J. B. *Fundamental psychiatry* (Rev. Ed.). Milwaukee: Bruce, 1966. Ch. XXVIII "Psychiatry, Philosophy, and Religion."

Cochrane, A. C. *The existentialists and God.* Philadelphia: Westminster Press, 1956. Introduction.

Coulson, C. A. *Science and Christian belief.* Chapel Hill: University of North Carolina Press, 1955. Ch. 4. "Christian Belief."

Cox, H. *The secular city.* New York: Macmillan, 1966. Ch. 9. "Sex and Secularization."

du Noüy, L. *Human destiny.* New York: Longmans, Greene, 1947. Ch. 13. "Religion—True Religion Is in the Heart;" Ch. 14. "The Idea of God and of Omnipotence."

Fremantle, Anne (Ed.) *A treasury of early Christianity.* New York: Viking, 1953. Part One. "The Christian Ideal."

Gleason, R. W. *The search for God.* New York: Sheed & Ward, 1964. Part I. "The Problem of God"; Part II. "The Denial of God."

Havens, J. *Psychology and religion: A contemporary dialogue.* Princeton: Van Nostrand. 1968. Ch. 1. "Varieties of God in the Psychologist's Frame of Reference"; Ch. 7. "Ethics and Values."

Hick, J. (Ed.) *The existence of God.* New York: Macmillan (paperback), 1964. Introduction; Part I, "The Theistic Arguments."

Hostie, R. *Religion and the psychology of Jung.* New York: Sheed & Ward, 1957. Ch. V. "The Psychology of Religion."

Jung, C. G. *Psychology and religion.* New York: Bollinger Foundation, 1958. "Psychotherapists or the Clergy" (pp. 327—347); "Psychoanalysis and the Cure of Souls" (pp. 348–354).

Kaufmann, W. A. *Existentialism from Dostoevsky to Sartre.* New York: Meridian, 1956. Ch. 1. "Kaufmann: Existentialism from Dostoevsky to Sartre."

Lawrence, N., and O'Connor, D. *Readings in existential phenomenology.* Englewood Cliffs: Prentice-Hall, 1967. Ch. 12. "Sex and Existence" (Van Kaam); Ch. 16. "The Experience of Happiness: A Phenomenological Typology" (Strasser).

Lewis, C. S. *The problem of pain.* London: Fontana (paperback), 1961. Ch. II. "Divine Omnipotence"; Ch. III. "Divine Goodness."

Lewis, C. S. *Mere Christianity.* New York: Macmillan, 1958. Preface; Book III, Ch. 5. "Sexual Morality"; Ch. 8. "The Great Sin"; Book IV. Ch. 11. "The New Men."

Mason, F. (Ed.) *The great design.* New York: Macmillan, 1935. "Introduction" (Thompson); "The Ascent of Mind" (Morgan); The Oneness and Uniqueness of Life" (MacBride).

May, R. (Ed.) *Symbolism in religion and literature.* New York: George Braziller, 1960. "Introduction: The Significance of Symbols" (May); Ch. 2. "The Religious Symbol' (Tillich).

Moore, T. V. *The life of man with God.* New York: Harcourt, Brace & World., 1956. Ch. X. "Penance and the Cross and the Joy of Life."

Pegis, A. C. *Basic writings of Saint Thomas Aquinas* (Vol. I). New York: Random House, 1944. "Question 2: The Existence of God."

Rahner, R. *Theological investigations. Vol IV. Later writings.* Baltimore: Helicon, 1966. Ch. 8. "Christology Within an Evolutionary View of the World."

Reinisch, L. (Ed.) *Theologians of our time.* South Bend: Notre Dame Press, 1964. "Karl Barth" (Wolf); "Rudolph Bultmann" (Wolf); "Emil Brunner" (Lohff); "Paul Tillich" (Burkle); "Reinhold Niebuhr" (Rohrbach); "Karl Adam" (Laubach).

Rokeach, M. *Beliefs, attitudes, and values.* San Francisco: Jossey-Bass, 1968. Ch. One. "The Organization and Modifications of Beliefs."

Sahakian, W. S., and Sahakian, M. L. *Realms of philosophy.* Chicago: Rand McNally, 1965. Ch. XX. "The Problem of God."

Schoonenberg, P. *God's world in the making*. Pittsburgh: Duquesne University Press, 1964. Ch. One. "Evolution."

Schrader, G. A. (Ed.) *Existential philosophers: Kierkegaard to Merleau-Ponty*. New York: McGraw-Hill, 1967. Ch. 1. "Existential Philosophy: Resurgent Humanism."

Teilhard de Chardin, P. *The future of man*. Harper & Row, 1965. Ch. X. "The Formation of the Noosphere"; Ch. XIX. "On the Probable Coming of an 'Ultra-Humanity.'"

Tillich, P. *The courage to be*. New Haven: Yale University Press, 1952. Ch. 6. "Courage and Transcendence."

Van der Veldt, J. H., and Odenwald, R. P. *Psychiatry and Catholicism*. New York: McGraw-Hill, 1952. Ch. 2. "The Moral Law, Conscience, and Responsibility"; Ch. 11. "Religion and Psychiatry."

Bibliography

Abbott, W. M. (Ed.) *The documents of Vatican II.* New York: Herder, 1966.

Abbott, W., Gilbert, A., Hunt, R., and Swaim, J. *The Bible reader: An interfaith interpretation.* New York: Bruce, 1969.

Adler, M. J. *The conditions of philosophy.* New York: Dell (Delta paperback), 1965.

Adler, M. J. *The difference of man and the difference it makes.* New York: World (Meridian paperback), 1968.

Alexander, A. F. *College apologetics.* Chicago: Regnery, 1954.

Alexander, A. F. *College moral theology.* Chicago: Regnery, 1957.

Allfrey, V. C., and Mirsky, A. E. *How cells make molecules.* Reprint from *Scientific American*, September 1961. San Francisco: Freeman, 1961.

Allport, F. H. *Theories of perception and the concept of structure.* New York: Wiley, 1955.

Allport, G. W. *Pattern and growth in personality.* New York: Holt, Rinehart and Winston, 1961.

Allport, G. *The person in psychology.* Boston: Beacon, 1968.

Altizer, T. *Toward a new Christianity: Readings in the death of God theology.* New York: Harcourt, Brace & World, 1967.

Arnold, M., and Gasson, J. *The human person.* New York: Ronald, 1954.

Ashby, W. R. *Design for a brain* (2d. Ed.). New York: Barnes & Noble, 1966.

Atkinson, J. W. *An introduction to motivation.* Princeton: Van Nostrand, 1964.

Ayer, A. J. *Language, truth, and logic.* New York: Dover, 1946.

Barbour, I. *Christianity and the scientist*. New York: Association, 1960.

Barbour, I. G. *Issues in science and religion*. Englewood Cliffs: Prentice-Hall, 1966.

Barbour, I. The significance of Teilhard. *Christian Century*, 1967, 84: 1090–1102.

Barrett, W. *Irrational man: A study in existential philosophy*. Garden City: Doubleday (paperback), 1958.

Barrett, W. *What is existentialism?* New York: Grove (paperback), 1964.

Barron, F. *Creative person and creative process*. New York: Holt, Rinehart and Winston (paperback), 1969.

Bernard, L. L. *Instinct: A study in social psychology*. New York: Holt, Rinehart and Winston, 1924.

Berofsky, B. *Free will and determinism*. New York: Harper & Row, 1966.

Bertalanffy, L. von *Robots, men, and minds: Psychology in the modern world*. New York: Braziller, 1967.

Bertalanffy, L. von *General systems theory: Essays on its foundation and development*. New York: Braziller, 1968.

Bindra, D. *Motivation*. New York: Ronald, 1959.

Bittle, C. N. *Reality and the mind: Epistemology*. Milwaukee: Bruce, 1936.

Bittle, C. N. *The domain of being: Ontology*. Milwaukee: Bruce, 1939.

Bittle, C. N. *From aether to cosmos: Cosmology*. Milwaukee: Bruce, 1941.

Bittle, C. N. *The whole man: Psychology*. Milwaukee: Bruce, 1945.

Bittle, C. N. *Man and morals: Ethics*. Milwaukee: Bruce, 1950.

Bittle, C. N. *The science of correct thinking: Logic*. Milwaukee: Bruce, 1950.

Blackham, H. J. (Ed.) *Reality, man, and existence: Essential works of existentialism*. New York: Bantam (paperback), 1965.

Blatt, B., and Kaplan, F. *Christmas in purgatory*. New York: Allyn & Bacon, 1967.

Boring, E. G. *A history of experimental psychology* (2d Ed.) New York: Appleton-Century-Crofts, 1950.

Boring, E. G. When is behavior pre-determined? *Scientific Monthly*, 1957, 84: 189–196.

Borzaga, R. *Contemporary philosophy*. Milwaukee: Bruce, 1966.

Bourke, V. J. *Ethics*. New York: Macmillan, 1951.

Boylan, M. E. *This tremendous lover*. Westminster, Md.: Newman, 1954.

Brachet, J. *The living cell*. Reprint from *Scientific American*, September 1961. San Francisco: Freeman, 1961.

Breisach, E. *Introduction to modern existentialism*. New York: Grove (paperback) 1962.

Bridgman, P. W. *The logic of modern physics*. New York: Macmillan, 1927.

Bube, R. (Ed.) *The encounter between Christianity and science*. Grand Rapids: Eerdmans, 1968.

Buber, M. *I and thou*. New York: Scribner's, 1958.

Buber, M. *Knowledge of man*. New York: Harper & Row (Torchbook paperback), 1965.

Bugental, J. F. T. *Challenges of humanistic psychology*. New York: McGraw-Hill, 1967.

Buhler, C., and Massarik, F. (Eds.) *Humanism and the course of life: Studies in goal-determination*. New York: Springer, 1968.

Camus, A. *The fall*. New York: Random House, 1956.

Camus, A. *The stranger*. New York: Random House (Vintage paperback), 1954.

Carol, J. B. (Ed.) *Mariology*. Vol I. *History of Mariology*. Milwaukee: Bruce, 1955.

Carol, J. B. *Fundamentals of Mariology*. New York: Benziger, 1956.

Carol, J. B. (Ed.) *Mariology*. Vol. II. *Theology of Mary*. Milwaukee: Bruce, 1957.

Carol, J. B. (Ed.) *Mariology*. Vol. III. *Devotion to Mary*. Milwaukee: Bruce, 1961.

Carrell, A. *Man the unknown*. New York: Harper & Row, 1935.

Cavanagh, J. R., and McGoldrick, J. B. *Fundamental psychiatry* (Rev. Ed.). Milwaukee: Bruce, 1966.

Chaplin, J. P., and Krawiec, T. S. *Systems and theories of psychology*. New York: Holt, Rinehart and Winston, 1960.

Cochrane, A. C. *The existentialists and God*. Philadelphia: Westminster, 1956.

Cofer, C. N., and Appley, M. H. *Motivation: Theory and research*. New York: Wiley, 1964.

Cole, W. G. *The restless quest of modern man*. New York: Oxford University Press, 1966.

Coleman, J. C. *Abnormal psychology and modern life* (3d Ed.). Glenview: Scott, Foresman, 1964.

Coleman, J. C. *Psychology and effective behavior*. Glenview: Scott, Foresman, 1969.

Compton, A. *The human meaning of science*. Chapel Hill: University of North Carolina Press, 1940.

Coulson, C. A. *Science and Christian belief*. Chapel Hill: University of North Carolina Press, 1955.

Cox. H. *The secular city*. New York: Macmillan, 1966.

Donceel, J. F. *Philosophical psychology* (2d Ed.). New York: Sheed & Ward, 1965a.

Donceel, J. F. Teilhard de Chardin: Scientist or philosopher? *International Philosophical Quarterly*, 1965b, 5: 248–266.

de Liguori, A. *The glories of Mary*. Brooklyn: Redemptionist Fathers, 1931.

du Noüy, L. *Human destiny*. New York: Longmans, Greene, 1947.

Evely, L. *Joy*. New York: Herder, 1968.

Feigl, H., and Sellars, W. (Eds.) *Readings in philosophical analysis*. New York: Appleton-Century-Crofts, 1949.

Francoeur, R. T. *Perspectives in evolution*. Baltimore: Helicon, 1965.

Frankl, V. E. *Man's search for meaning*. New York: Washington Square Press, 1963.

Frankl, V. E. *The doctor and the soul*. New York: Knopf, 1966.

Frankl, V. E. *Psychotherapy and existentialism.* New York: Washington Square Press, 1967.

Fremantle, Anne (Ed.) *A treasury of early Christianity.* New York: Viking, 1953.

Freud, S. *A general introduction to psychoanalysis.* Garden City: Doubleday, 1943.

Fromm, E. *The sane society.* New York: Holt, Rinehart and Winston, 1955.

Fromm, E. *The art of loving.* New York: Harper & Row (Torchbook paperback), 1956.

Fromm, E. *Escape from freedom.* New York: Holt, Rinehart and Winston, 1941 (also Avon Books, 1966).

Geldard, F. A. *Fundamentals of psychology.* New York: Wiley, 1962.

Gilula, M. F., Daniels, D. N., and Ochberg, F. M. *Violence and the struggle for existence.* Boston: Little, Brown, 1969.

Gilula, M. F., and Daniels, D. N. Violence and man's struggle to adapt. *Science,* 1969, 164: 396–405.

Gleason, R. W. *The search for God.* New York: Sheed & Ward, 1964.

Goodier, A. *The passion and death of Our Lord Jesus Christ.* New York: Kenedy, 1944.

Goulian, M., Kornberg, A., and Sinsheimer, R. L. Enzymatic synthesis of DNA. XXIV. Synthesis of infectious phage Phi X 174 DNA. *Proceedings of the National Academy of Sciences,* 1967, 58: 2321–2328.

Hall, C. S., and Lindzey, G. *Theories of personality.* New York: Wiley, 1957.

Hall, J. F. *Psychology of motivation.* Philadelphia, Lippincott, 1961.

Hammes, J. A. Our lady of mental health. *Friar,* March 1958, 6–11.

Hammes, J. A. *To help you say the Rosary better.* Paterson: St. Anthony Guild, 1962.

Hammes, J. A. *To help you follow the way of the cross.* Milwaukee: Bruce, 1964.

Hammes, J. A., Ahearn, T. R., and Keith, J. F. A chronology of two weeks' fallout shelter confinement. *Journal of Clinical Psychology,* 1965, 4: 452–456.

Hammes, J. A., Kelly, H. E., McFann, H. H., and Ward, J. S. *Technical report 41.* TRAINFIRE II: *A new course in basic technique of fire and squad tactics.* Washington: George Washington University Human Resources Research Office, 1957.

Hammes, J. A., and Osborne, R. T. Survival research in group isolation studies. *Journal of Applied Psychology,* 1965, 49: 418–421.

Hammes, J. A., and Osborne, R. T. Fallout shelter survival research. *Journal of Clinical Psychology,* 1966, 22: 344–346.

Hammes, J. A., Watson, J. A., Piercy, P. L., and Morgan, H. C. Environmentally confined groups on semi-starvation diets. *Psychological Reports,* 1965, 16: 1291–1292.

Havens, J. *Psychology and religion: A contemporary dialogue.* Princeton: Van Nostrand, 1968.

Hick, J. (Ed.) *The existence of God.* New York: Macmillan (paperback), 1964.

Hook, S. (Ed.) *Determinism and freedom.* New York: New York University Press, 1957.

Hook, S. (Ed.) *Dimensions of mind.* New York: New York University Press, 1959.

Horney, K. *Our inner conflicts.* New York: Norton, 1945.

Hostie, R. *Religion and the psychology of Jung.* New York: Sheed & Ward, 1957.

Hull, C. L. *Principles of behavior.* New York: Appleton-Century-Crofts, 1943.

Immergluck, L. Determinism-freedom in contemporary psychology: An ancient problem revisited. *American Psychologist*, 1964, 19: 270–281.

James, W. *The principles of psychology.* New York: Holt, Rinehart and Winston, 1890.

James, W. *Pragmatism.* New York: Longmans, Green, 1943.

Jeans, J. *The mysterious universe.* London: Cambridge University Press, 1931.

Jessor, R. The problem of reductionism in psychology. *Psychological Review*, 1958, 65: 170–178.

Jourard, S. M. *The transparent self: Self-disclosure and well-being.* Princeton: Van Nostrand (paperback), 1954.

Jung, C. G. *Psychology and religion.* New York: Bollingen Foundation, 1958.

Kaufmann, W. A. *Existentialism from Dostoevsky to Sartre.* New York: Meridian, 1956.

Kelly, W. L., and Tallon, A. *Readings in the philosophy of man.* New York: McGraw-Hill, 1967.

Kemp, C. G. *Intangibles in counseling.* Boston: Houghton Mifflin, 1967.

Keniston, K. *The uncommitted: Alienated youth in American society.* New York: Harcourt, Brace & World, 1965 (also Delta paperback, 1965).

Koch, S. (Ed.) *Psychology: A study of a science.* Vol. III. *Formulations of the person and the social context.* New York: McGraw-Hill, 1959.

Koch, S. (Ed.) *Psychology: A study of a science.* Vol V. *The process areas, the person, and some applied fields: Their place in psychology and in science.* New York: McGraw-Hill, 1963.

Lawrence, N., and O'Connor, D. *Readings in existential phenomenology.* Englewood Cliffs: Prentice-Hall, 1967.

Lewin, K. *A dynamic theory of personality.* New York: McGraw-Hill, 1935.

Lewis, C. S. *Mere Christianity.* New York: Macmillan, 1958.

Lewis, C. S. *The problem of pain.* New York: Macmillan, 1962.

Lindzey, G., and Hall, C. S. *Theories of personality: Primary sources and research.* New York: Wiley, 1965.

Long, E. *Religious beliefs of American scientists.* Philadelphia: Westminster, 1952.

MacCorquodale, K., and Meehl, P. E. On a distinction between hypothetical constructs and intervening variables. *Psychological Review*, 1948, 55: 95–107.

Madsen, K. B. *Theories of motivation.* Cleveland: Allen, 1961.

Marx, M. H., and Hillix, W. A. *Systems and theories in psychology*. New York: McGraw-Hill, 1963.

Maslow, A. H. *Toward a psychology of being*. Princeton: Van Nostrand (paperback), 1962.

Maslow, A. H. *The psychology of science: A reconnaissance*. New York: Harper & Row, 1966.

Mason, F. (Ed.) *The great design*. New York: Macmillan, 1935.

Matson, F. W. *The broken image: Man, science, and society*. New York: Braziller, 1964.

May, R. *The meaning of anxiety*. New York: Ronald, 1950.

May, R. *Man's search for himself*. New York: Norton, 1953.

May, R. (Ed.) *Symbolism in religion and literature*. New York: Braziller, 1960.

May, R. (Ed.) *Existential psychology*. New York: Random House, 1961.

May, R. *Psychology and the human dilemma*. Princeton: Van Nostrand, 1967.

May, R., Angel, E., and Ellenberger, H. F. (Eds.) *Existence*. New York: Simon & Shuster, 1967.

McFann, H. H., Hammes, J. A., and Taylor, J. E. *Technical report 22*. TRAINFIRE I: *A new course in basic rifle marksmanship*. Washington: George Washington University Human Resources Research Office, 1955.

Meissner, W. Intervening constructs: dimensions of controversy. *Psychological Review*, 1960, 67: 51–72.

Merton, T. *No man is an island*. New York: Harcourt, Brace & World, 1955.

Miller, N. E., et al. The frustration-aggression hypothesis: Symposium. *Psychological Review*, 1941, 48: 337–366.

Misiak, H., and Sexton, V. S. *History of psychology*: An overview. New York: Grune & Stratton, 1966.

Moore, R. *Evolution*. New York: Time, Life (Life Nature Library), 1964.

Moore, T. V. *Cognitive psychology*. Philadelphia: Lippincott, 1939.

Moore, T. V. *The driving forces of human nature and their adjustment*. New York: Grune & Stratton, 1948.

Moore, T. V. *The life of man with God*. New York: Harcourt, Brace & World, 1956.

Morgan, C. T. *Introduction to psychology* (2d Ed.) New York: McGraw-Hill, 1961.

Mowrer, O. H. *The crisis in psychiatry and religion*. Princeton: Van Nostrand, 1961.

Mowrer, O. H. *Morality and mental health*. Chicago: Rand McNally, 1967.

Pegis, A. C. *Basic writings of St. Thomas Aquinas* (Vol. I). New York: Random House, 1944.

Pius XII, Pope. *Mystici Corporis*. (Encyclical letter of Pope Pius XII on the Mystical Body of Christ.) Washington: National Catholic Welfare Conference, 1943.

Rahner, K. *Mary, mother of the Lord*. New York: Herder, 1963.

Rahner, K. *Theological investigations*. Vol. IV. *Later writings*. Baltimore: Helicon, 1966.

Raughley, R. *New frontiers of Christianity*. New York: Association, 1962.

Raymond, M. *God, a woman, and the way*. Milwaukee: Bruce, 1954.

Reinisch, L. (Ed.) *Theologians of our time*. Notre Dame, University of Notre Dame Press, 1964.

Rogers, C. R. *On becoming a person*. Boston: Houghton Mifflin, 1961.

Rokeach, M. *Beliefs, attitudes, and values*. San Francisco: Jossey-Bass, 1968.

Royce, J. E. *Man and his nature*. New York: McGraw-Hill, 1961.

Royce, J. E. *Man and meaning*. New York: McGraw-Hill, 1969.

Royce, J. R. *The encapsulated man: An interdisciplinary essay on the search for meaning*. Princeton: Van Nostrand, 1964.

Royce, J. R. (Ed.) *Psychology and the symbol*. New York: Random House, 1965.

Ruch, F. L. *Psychology and life* (7th Ed.) Chicago: Scott, Foresman, 1967.

Rychlak, J. *A philosophy of science for personality theory*. Boston: Houghton Mifflin, 1968.

Sahakian, W. S. *Psychology of personality: Readings in theory*. Chicago: Rand McNally, 1965.

Sahakian, W. S., and Sahakian, M. L. *Realms of philosophy*. Chicago: Rand McNally, 1965.

Schneiders, A. A. *Personality dynamics and mental health* (Rev. Ed.) New York: Holt, Rinehart and Winston, 1965.

Schoonenberg, P. *God's world in the making*. Pittsburgh: Duquesne, University Press, 1964.

Schoonenberg, P. *Man and sin*. Notre Dame: University of Notre Dame Press, 1965.

Schrader, G. A. (Ed.) *Existential philosophers: Kierkegaard to Merleau-Ponty*. New York: McGraw-Hill, 1967.

Severin, F. T. *Humanistic viewpoints in psychology*. New York: McGraw-Hill, 1965.

Shapley, H. *Science ponders religion*. New York: Appleton-Century-Crofts, 1960.

Sheehan, M. *Apologetics and catholic doctrine*. Dublin: Gill, 1949.

Sheen, F. J. *Lift up your heart*. Garden City: Doubleday (Image paperback), 1955.

Sheen, F. J. *Peace of soul*. Garden City: Doubleday (Image paperback), 1964.

Skinner, B. F. *Science and human behavior*. New York: Macmillan, 1953.

Smith, G. D. *The teaching of the Catholic Church* (Vols. I, II). New York: Macmillan, 1961.

Smith, K. The naturalistic conception of life. *American Scientist*, 1958, 46: 413–423.

Stevens, S. S. Psychology and the science of science. *Psychological Bulletin*, 1939, 36: 221–263.

Sutich, A., and Vich, M. (Eds.) *Readings in humanistic psychology*. New York: Free Press, 1969.

Tawney, R. H. *The acquisitive society*. New York: Harcourt, Brace & World, 1920.

Teilhard de Chardin, P. *The phenomenon of man*. New York: Harper & Row, 1959.

Teilhard de Chardin, P. *The future of man*. New York: Harper & Row, 1965.

Thomas à Kempis. *The imitation of Mary*. Westminster, Md.: Newman, 1954.

Tillich, P. *Systematic theology* (Vol. I). Chicago: University of Chicago Press, 1951.

Tillich, P. *The courage to be*. New Haven: Yale University Press, 1952.

Time. Education: Forth—without cheer. *Time*, June 27, 1960.

Turner, M. B. *Philosophy and the science of behavior*. New York: Appleton-Century-Crofts, 1965.

Turner, R. H. Dithering devices in the classroom: How to succeed in shaking up a campus by really trying. *American Psychologist*, 1966, 21 : 957–963.

Van der Veldt, J. H., and Odenwald, R. P. *Psychiatry and catholicism*. New York: McGraw-Hill, 1952.

Van Kaam, A. *Existential foundations of psychology*. Pittsburgh: Duquesne University Press 1966 (also Doubleday [paperback], 1969).

Vaughan, K. *The divine armory of Holy Scripture*. New York: Herder and Herder, 1957.

Wald, G. *The origin of life*. Reprint from *Scientific American*, September 1961. San Francisco: Freeman, 1954.

Wiener, N. *Cybernetics*. New York: Wiley, 1948.

Wolman, B. *Contemporary theories and systems in psychology* .New York: Harper & Row, 1960.

Woodworth, R. S., and Schlosberg, H. *Experimental psychology* (Rev. Ed.) New York: Holt, Rinehart and Winston, 1954.

Young, P. T. *Motivation and emotion*. New York: Wiley, 1961.

Index of Names

197

Chaplin, J. P., 49, 68, 70
Cochrane, A. C., 185
Cofer, C. N., 75, 76, 98
Cole, W. G., 38
Coleman, J. C., 88, 103, 133
Compte, A., 44
Compton, A., 164
Coulson, C. A., 38, 164, 185
Cox, H., 185

Democritus, 47
Descartes, R., 44, 46, 48, 164
DeVane, W. C., 108
Donceel, J. F., 17, 44, 52, 61, 98, 165
du Noüy, L., 98, 185

Empedocles, 47
Evely, L., 133

Fechner, G. T., 47, 73
Feigl, H., 17, 30
Francoeur, R. T., 56, 62, 98, 165
Frank, P., 17
Frankl, V. E., 133
Franklin, B., 19
Freemantle, A., 174, 185
Freud, S., 94
Fromm, E., 108, 133

Gasson, J., 97, 98, 132
Geldard, F. A., 70
Geulincx, A., 44, 47
Gilula, M. F., 7
Gleason, R. W., 25, 185
Goheen, R. F., 108
Goodier, A., 170
Gould, S. B., 109
Goulian, M., 61

Haeckel, E. H., 44, 47
Hall, C. S., 18, 20, 38, 48, 49, 51, 65,
   83, 98
Hammes, J. A., 14, 170, 182
Havens, J., 186
Hegel, G. W. F., 44, 47
Hick, J., 186
Hillix, W., 38, 43

Hobbes, T., 47
Hook, S., 98
Horney, K., 133
Hostie, R., 186
Hull, C. L., 78, 94
Hume, D., 35, 70

Immergluck, L., 85

James, W., 18, 50
Jaspers, K., 10
Jeans, J., 164
Jessor, R., 36
Jourard, S. M., 133
Jung, C. G., 48, 186

Kant, I., 44, 47, 138
Kaplan, F., 56
Kaufmann, W. A., 186
Keith, J., 14
Kemp, C. G., 9, 133
Keniston, K., 6, 133
Kierkegaard, S., 162
Koch, S., 43
Krawiec, T., 49, 68, 70

Lawrence, N., 38, 98, 186
Leibnitz ,G. W., 44, 47
Lewin, K., 43, 94
Lewis, C. S., 186
Lindzey, G., 18, 20, 38, 48, 49, 51, 65,
   83, 98
Locke, J., 70

MacCorquodale, K., 36
McFann, H. H., 14
McGoldrick, J., 133, 185
Madsen, K. B., 99
Malebranche, N., 44, 47
Marx, M. H., 38, 43
Maslow, A. H., 38, 134
Mason, F., 164, 186
Massarik, R., 133
Matson, F. W., 4, 38, 99
May, R., 7, 10, 38, 99, 104, 105, 106,
   107, 134, 186
Meehl, P., 36

Index of Subjects